# The Pig in the Pantry
## And Other Homeschool Tales

*Rose Godfrey*

The Pig in the Pantry and Other Homeschool Tales.
Copyright © 2011 by Rose Godfrey

*The Pig in the Pantry and Other Homeschool Tales* is adapted from the *Learning at Home* column written by Rose Godfrey. *Learning at Home* appears in the *Appeal-Democrat* in Marysville, CA. The title essay originally appeared in *Home Education Magazine*, November, 2004.

Cover Art J. Simmons, www.jsimmonsillustration.com

ISBN-13: 978-1466350403
ISBN-10: 1466350407

www.rosegodfrey.com

Special thanks to Brian for daily making my dreams come true, to my children for helping me to discover the wonder in every day life, to Daisy Philipp for reminding me to follow a dream, and to Susan Benitez and Michael Green at the *Appeal-Democrat* for years of editorial support.

# The Pig in the Pantry
## And Other Homeschool Tales

## Table of Contents

Part Five: Farm Life

Part Six: Family

# Introduction

# Will the Real Homeschoolers Please Stand Up?

How to homeschool is an ongoing topic of debate within the homeschool community. It goes deeper than how to teach science or whether to use workbooks or unit studies. Some people bicker over the meaning of the word homeschool itself.

In an online homeschool forum, a member of the Can't-We-All-Get-Along Crowd suggested using the term "homeschool hybrid" as a way to describe homeschooling that has any regulatory strings attached to it. This suggestion garnered instant unity—it was condemned from all sides.

There are those I call the purists—they were homeschooling when homeschooling wasn't cool. In some states, the purists fought for, and won, the right to educate their children at home. They are active in preserving and promoting the rights and the practices of homeschooling. For the most part, they aren't about to share the word "homeschool" with a bunch of Johnny-come-lately charter schoolers.

The purists point out that there have been many irresponsible groups that have come along and used homeschooling as just another marketing ploy, ignoring the educational needs of children to make a buck.

In fact, the purists have always kept a pretty wary eye on those who used any sort of oversight body to monitor or add requirements to homeschooling. Before charter schools came along there were correspondence classes, religious groups and private schools that would, for a fee, have a teacher make assignments, grade school work and maintain records and transcripts. All of those entities still exist, but charter schools are leading the pack when it comes to enrolling students.

Ask a charter school student who is enrolled in a home study program where he goes to school, and most likely he will say, "I'm homeschooled." Ask a purist about that and she will explain that the child is doing public school at home. The purist has a point.

Charter schools are public schools. Children enrolled in them are students of a public school. As such, they adhere to state standards and laws regarding education of children enrolled in the school. Charter schools use public funds from our tax dollars to pay for teachers, textbooks, supplies and field trips, just as traditional public schools do.

Many families find charter schools to be a good fit. The school maintains the structure and records for each child's education. A teacher assigns and oversees a child's assignments, and the parents are responsible for the bulk of the instruction. There is support available for those who are not comfortable or for those who feel only minimally qualified to teach. Not having to purchase curriculum is a big draw, too.

The purists would argue that accepting publicly-funded materials as for a child's education defies what they have fought for and places us all at risk of losing the right to homeschool independently. With government money comes government strings.

Charter schoolers would argue that they are teaching their children at home—what else would you call it besides homeschooling? To take it further, isn't this what it is all about—the freedom to educate as a family sees fit? If a family chooses the regulations that come with a publicly-funded program, does that choice count as one of those rights the purists fought to obtain?

The debate goes on.

# Hallelujah, I'm a Homeschooler

I never intended to homeschool. We just happened to adopt a couple kids who were 9 and 10 years old. Three weeks of public schooling prompted me to give homeschooling a try. In my professional life—whatever that means—I am a speech pathologist. I was just gutsy enough to think that if I could teach people to speak for a living, I could educate my children and teach them English.

It was supposed to be a temporary solution, but homeschooling fit our family like a favorite pair of jeans, comfy in all the right places. As the children kept coming, by birth and by additional adoptions, we stayed the course.

Over the years, I have worked on a number of public school campuses. When I was there, I was a triple outsider, a contractor in special education who homeschools. I often ended up going to several schools each week, and when I got to my assigned room, I needed to rustle up pens, pencils, paper and other basic supplies just to do my job.

Some days I wanted to sit around the fireplace with the students and read stories or take a walk in the yard, stopping to chase a bug or pick some fruit, just as I do with my own children, but this was not possible. My day was regimented by bells and scheduled accordingly. I saw dozens of children and then filled out the paperwork to prove it.

I have found many excellent and dedicated people working in the schools where I have worked, but institutionalized, mass-market education cannot meet the unique needs of each child. While some are nurtured and encouraged, others barely get by, and still others lose their spark of creativity.

The asphalt jungle sprouts few trees, none suitable for climbing. Many types of play structures are now banned, citing the various dangers that may be present. Instead of training children to be careful, we take away the opportunity to learn safety in a natural environment. At recess, staff remind children of the dangers of chasing or playing tag.

I have seen time outs for saying "hallelujah" and lines that can't move forward until everyone's feet are pointed in the same direction. Who cares which way a kid points his feet while standing in line? How, I ask myself, does this enhance learning?

Hallways lined with posters about saving the environment lead to the cafeteria that tells a different story. Students pick up a plastic-lined paper tray then fill it with a foil-wrapped bun, a dried-out hamburger patty in a shrink-wrapped plastic bowl, condiments, boxed fruit, small cartons of milk and another shrink-wrapped bowl filled with lettuce.

The children rip apart containers and pick at their food. Some eat, and you realize this may be the most reliable means of nutrition available to them. Others throw their meals in the trash in favor of chips and cookies stashed in a backpack. I always found myself wondering what the ecology lesson really is here. Sure, some schools have recycling programs for their green and paper waste, but why not avoid using those extra resources in the first place?

I see all of this and more, and I am grateful to homeschool. While I realize that homeschooling is not for everyone, I would like to see more people give it a try. Even as that happens, there is still no quick fix for those children left behind in the abyss of public education, pointing their feet in the wrong direction, saying "hallelujah" and heading off to time out.

# Part One

# Motherhood

The mother-child relationship is paradoxical and, in a sense, tragic. It requires the most intense love on the mother's side, yet this very love must help the child grow away from the mother, and to become fully independent.
~Erich Fromm

# Just Call Me Mom

One fall day, 6-year-old Bella slipped her hand into mine as we walked, her presence breaking into my solemn musings. Her hands are always hot. Like her father, she radiates heat. She chattered along, unconcerned about putting food on the table or repairing the porch. She did not know what a mortgage is, so she certainly did not think about paying one. No, she chattered on about bird tracks and horses and wondered aloud where trucks go when they are full of rocks.

I start to explain about how the rocks were going to make new roads. She was interested for a moment. "You could make a lot of roads here," she said, pointing to the gravel in our driveway. And then she was off on another topic.

"Can I run?" she asked, and I sent her on her way. She did not run that day because it is good for her heart or because high impact exercise will increase her bone density. She ran because she was a child on a clear fall day, and it simply felt good to sprint.

After a moment, she took a detour to look for bird tracks, but she did not find any. That day, I decided to play along. Paying bills and fixing dinner could wait. Soon we were both sloshing through soaked leaves, looking for bird

2

tracks. "I'll find them before you will," I challenged. "Oh, no you won't!" she shrieked, and she was off, giggling and dashing as I chased her. I dropped my worries and enjoyed the simple pleasure of playing with my daughter.

This, I told myself, is what unschooling was meant to be. I wondered how to preserve this moment forever. Again, Bella cut into my reverie.

"HeyLookMom!"

She was running again, pointing to a persimmon clinging to the tree we planted together a few years back. "We gotta show Dad!" Bird tracks and trucks full of rocks were forgotten as she dashed in with her discovery. "LookDad!" she hollered. We used to be called Brian and Rose, but as parents we became LookDad and HeyLookMom.

I once tried not answering unless my kids only called me Mom, but I couldn't remember to keep quiet when they called something else. Sophia cleared it all up. "Your name is Mom," she informed me, "but your nickname is Rose."

The first time anyone called me "Mama," I was in Russia. My children, with their thick accents, were trying to get my attention, but I didn't even recognize the word as being connected to me. It was all too new. The translator laid her hand on my arm and gently whispered, "They are calling you." Mama. Oh, yes, I am Mama. I wanted to look around for an instruction manual, but there wasn't time.

I considered telling them the truth: I was an imposter. I did not know the first thing about being a mother. I was still in shock that the judge had not figured this out. Instead, she had smiled, nodded and signed the adoption decrees. If I had faked her out, maybe I could fake the kids out. "Fake it 'til you make it" became my motto.

Years later, I answer to anything. I find myself mumbling "What, Honey?" to any child calling out within a 3-aisle range in the grocery store. Odds are, the kid is mine. I'm just covering my bases.

When the babies came along, I would delight in their first attempts at saying "Mama." Other names came soon enough. Max briefly figured out that calling me Rose got my attention. If it was good enough for his Daddy to do it, it must be a good idea.

Time passed, as it always does. The boy who first called me "Mama" in a Russian orphanage grew up to be a man and headed off to boot camp. After a few weeks, he wrote a letter home. "Hey, Mom," the letter began.

My son's letter informed me that he had to do pushups for every letter received. I smiled and wrote back right away. Three times.

It is bittersweet to get a letter from a grown-up child. I found myself asking where the time went. How could I possibly have adult children? They must belong to that aging woman who peered out from the mirror each morning.

Years ago, a family friend called me to complain that her grandson had just turned 50. "How could he be 50? That is so old," she told me. I may not be as far along as she is, but I understand her point in my own way. They keep growing up.

I feel like I've been holding my breath for so long. "Breathe, breathe," they told me when I was in labor. I thought it was advice for just that moment. Turns out I keep needing to remember to exhale. I held my breath as I watched a son take a first step. I held my breath as a daughter crossed the street alone. I held my breath as another teen learned to drive. Breathe. Breathe.

A good friend watched her son go through a series of surgeries, the first one when he was a few days old. It is an anxiety I do not know. Another friend lost a baby when he was only a few months old. It is a pain I have never felt. As mothers, we share a common name, a common bond. We are moms.

Of all the things I've ever been called—and I best not list all of them here—I am the proudest when I hear my favorite of them all: Mom.

# Collective Bargaining at Home

Even as a confirmed homeschooling mom, I often think of the downsides of teaching my own children. I've forgotten what it means to be alone. Our house maintains a certain lived-in look all the time. Those are small inconveniences that I have learned to deal with. The biggest problem with homeschooling is that I can't sue anybody if I mess up.

All the talk about collective bargaining for teachers set me to thinking about my rights, responsibilities and current working conditions as a homeschooling mom.

In our homeschool, collective bargaining is a little different than it is in the public sector. Around here, collective bargaining might be a good description of how the kids gang up on me, lobbying for the perks they feel they deserve. It is a process that never ends. There are calls for longer and more frequent recess breaks. Skipping homework, watching movies, and eating a nonstop buffet of sweets are other topics on the bargaining table.

Perhaps I don't fully understand the concept of collective bargaining. A quick Google search showed me some of the benefits that unions negotiate for their employees.

My main beef, of course, is working hours. School is always in session, and my students are always with me. Management reminds me that our actual hands-on book time is less than what it might be in a traditional school. Score one for management. I am also reminded that I get to go on field trips at my discretion. I can choose who goes and who stays, too. Another plus, duly noted.

Class size is another sticking point I'd encounter as a public employee in contract negotiations. I've got a great plan in that regard, one I don't want to give up. Classroom management is a breeze.

I might be inclined to discuss improving my wages if I actually had any. I guess you could say I'm on a delayed compensation plan: My pay can't be measured in terms of a bank account.

Contributing to my retirement plan is simple, too, as long as I don't need to actually pitch in money. I contribute toward my plan every day—baking cookies, kissing owies and teaching responsibility along with our math and history lessons. Then I tell my children that I expect them to take care of me in my old age. They can't argue with their mouths full of cookies.

Still, there are workplace safety issues to be considered. If I am the head teacher, then Brian is the administration department. As such, it is his responsibility to look out for the welfare of his staff (me).

I thought about this one day as I was standing just inside the pig pasture. The pigs like to root around and one of their favorite hobbies seems to be digging around the fence line, damaging the fence. Brian solved this problem by running a line of electrical rope around the bottom perimeter of the fence. At the gate, the electric rope comes up and over the top of the gate then down again.

I helped Brian with part of the fencing. I stood back when we turned it on, and I watched as the pigs tested the fence. The problem is, Brian never specifically said, "Rose, you should not put your elbow on the electric rope fence when it is on because it will shock you, and that will hurt." Furthermore, he did not advise me that holding on to a metal gate while touching the electric rope would conduct the electricity in such a way as to make me remember this lesson for the rest of my natural life.

If he were a real school administrator and not my husband, I could sue him for that. See? This is a real downfall in home education.

Around the same time that this happened, I read the story of 18-year-old Kyle Dubois of Dover, New Hampshire. Kyle attended a regular public school where he was in an electrical trades class.

Apparently, the teacher did not clearly say, "Kyle, if you hook up an alligator clip to one nipple and have a friend hook the cord to the other nipple while a third teenager plugs in the cord, it will hurt you really badly." As a result of this egregious oversight, Kyle and his friends did, in fact, plug Kyle in to an outlet while the teacher was talking with another student. And it hurt. The paramedics had to restart Kyle's heart and he needed brain surgery to relieve the swelling in his brain.

I took an informal poll of my kids to ask what they thought Kyle's parents would have told him. I try to instill a touch of common sense, so I had to see if anyone had been listening.

Olivia thought Kyle's parents probably said, "I feel sorry for you." Bella was more direct. Her response was, "That was really stupid."

Alyona, as the older and wiser of the bunch, gave the answer Kyle's parents chose: "We'll sue the school." Apparently, the basis of the lawsuit was that Kyle was not specifically warned that electrical cords can be dangerous. And they claim he has brain damage. Now, not before.

Sadly, defending the school against this will cost the district, and ultimately the taxpayers, money. That reality is precisely the reason I can't sue Brian over any of my working conditions—I would just end up getting the bill.

# Homeschool Mom Just Wants to Have Fun

I thought fairy godmothers only appeared in story books and movies, but it isn't so. I have one. Apparently, fairy godmothers are in cahoots with the postal service to deliver their messages of good cheer. My fairy godmother sent me a welcome delivery.

We have a lot of projects started here. Sometimes the planning and the set up are more interesting than the daily routines that follow to keep those ventures running. It is exciting to order a couple hundred chicks and plan for their arrival, but the new wears off pretty quickly for all of us. I was thinking about that as I walked back in from feeding some of the critters. It was a pleasant day, perfectly ordinary, with nothing in particular to set it apart from any other day. Then the mail came.

My mysterious letter from my fairy godmother contained a short note instructing me to have fun and a stipend that insured that I could follow through on that plan.

I decided that my fun time would be time just for me. Maybe I was being selfish, but I sensed that this note came from someone who knew that wiping noses and bottoms can be a thankless job. Someone, perhaps, who had walked a mile in my size 11s. I owed it to both of us to take some time for myself. I just had to plan my adventure.

With a large family, I don't get a lot of opportunity to be alone. The last time someone used the word "privacy" in a sentence, I had to look it up in the dictionary to remember what it meant.

A friend's mom used to keep a can of soda in the tank of the toilet, assuming that her children would never look there. When she had a chance, she'd slip in with a glass of ice, pop the top on the can and have a few minutes to herself. I thought this was absurd until I had children.

The bathroom hasn't turned out to be much of a haven for me. A few years back, we stopped at a chocolate factory for a tour. The day stood out in my mind because it was the first time in a few years that I felt comfortable leaving my little ones outside the bathroom stall. As I contemplated this small victory, I heard a 3-year-old voice and looked up to see my daughter peering under the stall door. "Mo-om, I see you!"

Even at home, I can't skip off to the loo. Someone always finds me, even though I tell them, "I'm going in the bathroom alone. Do not bother me unless there is an emergency."

This is, of course, a clear signal to my children that I want to spend time with them.

Knock, knock, knock.

"Are you bleeding?"

"No, but, Mom..."

"Is anyone else bleeding?"

"No, but Mom, I really need you."

"OK, what is it?"

"What comes after 56?"

"Go ask your father!"

I heard Olivia run out to find Brian.

"Dad, what comes after 56? I already asked Mom. She doesn't know either."

A few weeks passed before I went out and had my fairy-godmother-inspired fun day. Part of the enjoyment came from plotting possibilities. I scheduled a spa day where nobody peeked under the door and nobody asked for help with school work. On the way home, I bought an ice cream cone and ate it without sharing so much as one lick.

Thank you, Fairy Godmother.

# Part Two

## Curriculum

"I have never let my schooling interfere with my
education."
~Mark Twain

A person has to be pretty brave to come and stay at our place. The closest thing to the Ritz around here is a couple of crackers that somehow found their way under the couch. Look closer and you may find a stray flip flop and assorted toys under there too. Plus, we live in the country, a good distance from any major tourist attractions. I think we'd get more visitors if we lived around the corner from Disneyland. Out in the yard, a visitor may find children chasing lizards, swinging from a tree or cooking up a water fight. Not exactly E-ticket attractions.

I count myself blessed to have a few friends who are willing to overlook the shortcomings of the accommodations and come to visit. My friend Robbi was brave enough to fly cross-country for an extended visit. Twice.

"This will be interesting," my friend told me. I nodded silently. She had no idea.

When she got here, Robbi wanted to know abut homeschooling. "How do you homeschool?" she asked. "What do the kids do all day?" They are common questions, and I often explain that our days never look the same. In our home, we do have a structured and comprehensive curriculum for third grade and up, and the children pretty much choose when they will work on those subjects. Other times, learning is more fluid. Education starts in infancy and continues for a lifetime. The stories in this section show a few examples of how we have included academic lessons into everyday life.

# Reading with Sicily

Sicily laid her head on my chest and snuggled in. I would have relished this moment a little more if it didn't come at such a price. Usually this child fights against sleep, but this time her little body was hot, and she settled into a feverish nap for as long as my arms would hold her. And I wanted to hold her because she needed me, but also because I sensed that snuggling days are precious and short. Soon enough she will tell me she is too big to cuddle.

Besides, homeschoolers can't call in sick. We are already home. Even sickness provides an opportunity as we teach our kids to listen to their bodies, keep hydrated and get some rest. Often that rest time is spent curled up with a book as the body heals. As I held my little one, I knew that soon the baby would be back to her explorations.

On the eve of her first birthday, Sicily was into everything. She would stand and think about walking, then decide she would rather crawl or let someone carry her.

I liked to sit and watch her and I became fascinated all over again at the way a child develops. We had been through this stage many times before. She was not the first to empty out the bottom cabinets or to pull all the wipes out of the container. It was all new to her, though, and she delighted in each new discovery. "Look at this!" she told us all with her smile. She chattered away in her own little way, and we responded as if we were having a regular conversation. Sicily didn't know it yet, but she was developing pre-literacy skills.

Homeschooling starts early around here, and our version of education always includes books. There are many methods out there to teach children to read. As a speech pathologist, I can tell you many reasons a child doesn't learn to read. I can toss out some technical jargon that explains away a multitude of problems, but when it comes down to how kids learn literacy skills, I am still just in awe of the process. It is a miracle. That miracle can be coaxed along with a little help.

A love of reading starts by having something to read. We have books, magazines and newspapers everywhere in our house.

A few years ago, a friend asked if she could give us some books her children had finished. We were blessed with four boxes of new-to-us books, and we were all delighted.

The kids stayed busy for weeks. The younger ones held their books upside down and begged the older ones to read them out loud. New favorites were found each day, and there were piles of books all over the house. Eventually, they all made their way into overflowing bookshelves.

Sicily's first taste of solid food was a page out of a book. She had taken several bites before anyone noticed what she was up to. What can I say? It was a good book.

A year passed, and her interest in books grew. Sicily began to understand that each book held a piece of imagination, and she wanted in on the action.

"Mom! Bee!"

Her bare feet slapped on the hardwood floor as she ran to me. She shoved a tattered copy of *Winnie the Pooh and Tigger Too* at me. "Bee!" she demanded.

At nearly 2, Sicily could not quite coax the little muscles in her tongue and lips to form sounds correctly. She enthusiastically tried her best, and it was up to me to study the context and interpret her attempts at communication. In those early days, "beewee" meant "baby," and "wee" meant "drink." My little talker used new words every day, delighted in her ability to direct her world using her words. "Bee," when announced with a book in hand was Sicily's version of "read."

Babies begin to communicate shortly after birth, and it all starts coming together when the true words begin to flow. There was not much time for me to think it over. My daughter expected my immediate attention. "Bee!" she reminded me.

I reached to take the book from my daughter and she snatched it away. "Mine!" she said as she screeched and ran off again, delighted to express her independence.

Moments later she returned, still running. In her arms she carried her favorite book, *Go Away, Big Green Monster!* by Ed Emberley. Sicily handed it to me, and I expected her to snatch this one away too. "Bee!" she commanded. She climbed onto my lap. "Up!" she announced.

I opened the book and read the words I had read enough times to memorize. "Big Green Monster has two big yellow eyes," I began. My daughter looked up at me and smiled, as if we were sharing a secret. I continued reading. Her favored book had cut outs on each page, each one revealing a new aspect of the monster.

I read about Big Green Monster's little squiggly ears and purple scraggly hair. Sicily giggled at each page. In the middle of the book, we declared our fearlessness together. "You don't scare me, Big Green Monster!" I growled. The giggles multiplied.

My daughter was delighted to control my attention for a few moments. She did not know we were laying the foundation for learning to read. It did not occur to her that her education had already begun there in the recliner as she snuggled in my lap.

We turned the pages together as I now commanded the monster to vanish, one part at a time. "Go away, sharp white teeth," I said. "Go away, long bluish greenish nose."

Sicily echoed me, yelling "Way!" and pointing her finger at the monster. Finally, the monster was gone. "And don't come back," I continued reading, "until I say so." I closed the book.

"Mine!" she said, and grabbed the book away from me. She flipped the pages randomly, jabbering to herself. Occasionally she began yelling and wagging her fingers at the monster. Her storytelling was a whole body experience. Little toes flexed and curled with delight.

I was no longer allowed to touch the book, but I was required to pay attention as she told me the story. If I looked away or resumed reading my magazine, my daughter redirected my attention by pulling my face closer to hers. "Mom, bee!" Sicily reminded me.

She hopped down and ran away, cradling her book in her arms. The activities of the older children caught her attention, and she scampered off to see what mischief she could find with them. Reading time was done, and I was left with a happy memory of precious time well spent.

# Spelling with Bella

Bella discovered spelling when she was 3 years old.

"What else starts with 'u'?" she asked. "Underwear," I replied, without turning away from my writing. She sighed. Loudly.

"No, Mom, not 'u', what else starts with 'you'. You know, like 'Mom'."

We were clearly not having the same conversation.

I looked up from my computer to find Bella sprawled on the living room floor, a discarded computer keyboard in one hand and a number two pencil in the other. She was using the pencil to point at me, demonstrating the spelling differences I obviously did not understand. "What can I write that starts with 'you'?"

"How about 'Mommy'?" I asked.

She sighed again. "I already wrote Mom."

"Yes, but 'Mommy' has a 'y' at the end."

That kept her happy and occupied for about two seconds before she started rattling off a series of other letters or words that she wanted me to spell for her.

I watched as she patiently found the letters on the keyboard and either pressed them or copied them onto her paper. The only spelling rule she observed was one of her own making: No letters could be repeated until all of them had been used. It was up to me to think up words for her, but I never seemed to live up to her rigorous standard, and she quickly became exasperated with my ineptitude.

Some days, she would have made me a dunce cap and put me in the corner, but she kept me around because I do have a few other uses. For the most part, she finds me entertaining, or at least tolerable, depending on the day. I'm good for an occasional drive to the park, a snuggle and a few snacks.

Fortunately, her interest in spelling in those days was usually short-lived, and she soon was ready to go outside and swing, which brought up another of my uses. I am a great swing pusher.

"Higher! Higher!" she commanded. Pushing Bella on the swing was one of my more important functions, second only to my hot chocolate making ability. I told her my hot chocolate is better than anyone else's because I put love in it, and she believed me. It is nice to be needed, if only for a moment.

When Bella was 4, we played "Ringman", her version of Hangman. Once, on a road trip, the older kids had started a game of paperless Hangman in the van, and Bella thought it was great fun. She was ready to play Ringman any time we headed down the driveway.

"OK, Mom," she'd holler from her booster seat near the back of the van, "I've got five letters. It's your turn." At this point, I was supposed to call out a letter, "as long as it's not a 'K'," she'd warn. "I can't make 'K'." Sometimes the other kids were invited to play, other times not. She never quite trusted them to get it right. After I'd toss a few letters her way, she would instruct me to guess the word.

Soon Bella was a beginning reader. On her first day of kindergarten at home, she was bitterly disappointed that she didn't learn to read all in one day. Reading was harder than it looked. Once she realized that spelling was part of school, she relaxed. After all, she'd had years of practice.

# Olivia Loves Math

"Get your chores done NOW," I said, "or I will not let you do any more pages in your math book today." I never thought I'd tell any of my kids that one. My oldest once asked if there was math in heaven. She was lobbying against it. Olivia was a different story. Her math book was a reward.

Born in her sister's shadow, Olivia learned to be persistent in order to be heard. Her requests for a real math book were loud and frequent. When her workbook finally arrived, she was ecstatic.

"She's excited about math?" My teen was incredulous. It just didn't seem possible that anyone could beg for more math, but it was happening right there before our eyes.

Olivia opened her book and caressed the page. She grabbed her pencil and got to work. A short while later, I looked over to see her busily working with a calculator.

"Wait a minute. You can't use a calculator," I informed her. Her face fell. "But this is subtraction, Mommy. I can't do subtraction. I need someone to help me."

I assured her that I could teach her to subtract without a calculator. Her eyes narrowed as she thought about that. She had seen me balance the checkbook. I used the calculator, and I muttered a lot, so she couldn't really be sure that I knew what I was talking about. She decided to give it a shot.

I sent her off to grab a handful of crayons—the closest set of 10 objects she could find. Olivia quickly understood the concept of subtraction using manipulatives and dismissed me. That first night, she stayed up late with her math book. By the next morning, she had finished 35 pages, and I had to threaten to take her workbook away so she could get something else done.

It wasn't always like this. Olivia hit her developmental milestones late. At 16 months, she still wasn't crawling. Instead, she sat on her bottom and used her foot to scoot herself along. I contemplated taking her to a pediatric physical therapist, and then suddenly she started crawling. A few days later, she took her first steps. I worried about that too, concerned that gaps in her learning sequence might be signs of struggles yet to come.

It wasn't just the motor skills. She talked later than the other children had, and when she finally started using words, hardly anyone could understand what she was saying. As a speech pathologist, I knew that children who mispronounce multiple sounds often have trouble with phonics later. I kept a close eye on her speech production.

As she grew, Olivia stayed within the range of normal, but always at the lower end. Colleagues reminded me to have patience and let her develop at her own pace. That sort of advice is so much easier to give than to take.

We enrolled her in ballet and hoped it would help her coordination. At home, we read to her and had her imitate sounds. I wondered how she would learn to read. Kindergarten passed uneventfully.

The summer before first grade, my daughter started picking up books and sounding out words. She followed everyone around, asking for help. She turned over a bucket and read to me while I milked the cow. Olivia fell in love with reading.

Then she discovered math.

She chattered as she worked on another math page. "Eight minus four is four," she told me. "This is too easy, Mom, I think I need a second grade book."

I stopped worrying.

# Cookie Math

We often lean toward unschooling and away from traditional instruction methods, a task that requires us to define what each of those would be for ourselves and then pick and choose the parts that we think are going to work the best for our children.

For example, how does a child learn the times tables? This is a topic of endless discussion in our home. I learned to do multiplication by doing piles of timed drills. Other people learn by using flash cards.

Some now say that flash cards work the best when you present the entire problem ($5 \times 3 = 15$) on one card so that the child repeats the phrase for each one. In this manner, the child stores a visual and auditory memory of the entire equation and, the theory goes, the child is then better able to fill in the blank when presented with a problem on paper.

Other educators will tell you it is better to focus on the application of math and not so much on the facts. After all, kids start using calculators around kindergarten anyway, so what is the point of spending time in rote memory tasks?

I like to use cooking as a sneaky way to teach math. Teaching measurement and fractions just seems easier when there is a cookie at the end of the lesson. We can work in some language arts and some very basic chemistry as well. Learning the culinary arts starts early around here. As soon as a kid is old enough to hold a spoon, that child is old enough to be a cook's helper.

The duties of a cook's helper are varied. Stirring is easily mastered, then we move on, as age and interest allow, to measuring, kneading and chopping. Soon, they want to cook on their own.

Young children are delighted at the ability to make toast independently, and that desire for independence broadens with age to include frying eggs, making oatmeal and brewing tea. With the ability to read comes the ability to follow a simple recipe. Then the real fun begins.

The older girls can cook almost anything they set their minds to. The younger ones clamor to catch up. Sophia and Olivia have demonstrated the aptitude and interest to make cookies without a parent's intervention. Together, they divide up tasks. One creams butter and sugar while another measures flour. The evidence of their learning nurtures us all.

The challenge, at this point, is in preserving the novelty. They'd bake daily if I allowed it, and my waistline can't afford to keep up with grading all their work.

When the older children cook, the youngest ones have an opportunity to learn about equitable distribution of assets. Fairness is in the eye of the beholder, and the cookie count is serious business.

Atticus takes his learning seriously. As he was just on the cusp of 4, he insisted that he needed to have workbooks. He counted, he drew and he was determined to keep up with his older brother. It was only natural that all of this would come together when the girls made cookies.

After the first round of cookies and milk had been consumed, Atticus came to me, and we worked on his pre-math skills. He was after another cookie, and he was sure he had logic on his side.

"Mom, can I have a cookie?" he began. "I only had eleven and everyone else had two. Can I have two too?"

"You had eleven cookies?"

"Yeah, I had eleven. Can I have two now?"

"Honey, eleven is more than two. Are you sure you had eleven?"

He sighed. It is hard to put up with me sometimes, a point he made abundantly clear.

"Yes, I had eleven cookies. Can I have two like Max?"

"Eleven is almost the whole pan. Did you really have a whole pan of cookies?"

At this point, exasperation overcame the child.

He held up one index finger. "I had one." He held up the other index finger next to the first "Then I had one."

He moved the fingers close together so they were nearly touching. "See? Eleven." The logic was clear enough. "So can I have two cookies?"

I touched my finger to his raised index fingers, counting. "Well, one and one makes two, so you already had two cookies."

He looked at me patiently, hoping once again to explain. He pushed one hand toward my face, raised his middle finger to go with his index finger, forming a peace sign or, in this case, a two.

"No, Mom, this is two."

"So. Can I have a cookie now?"

Finding that I had no argument against such a stunning display of logic, I gave in. "Let's go," I said. "I'll pour the milk."

# Spring Testing

Spring is the time in public schools when the test booklets and number two pencils come out for another shot at judging how much a teacher has taught, how much a child has learned. Maybe some of that routine stuck with us because when the spring winds begin to blow, I start to ponder how we, as homeschoolers, measure up.

There are different ways to find out what a child has learned. With criterion-referenced testing, a teacher can try to determine if a child has mastered a specific skill—does a child know how to decipher a math problem, a recipe or the instructions for a science project? Does a child know how to look something up in the dictionary, the encyclopedia or on the Internet? Can a child spell a word or recite multiplication tables? These kinds of measurements are seen in every day assignments, quizzes, and ongoing assessments of learning.

When I want an official analysis of how my kids measure up, I've found that a quick check of the state standards for each grade can often put my mind at ease—or tell me where we need to get to work.

But I am a naturally competitive kind of person, and there is another kind of assessment that keeps me up some nights—the comparison of my children's skills to the skills of other people's children. Officially, it is called norm-referenced testing when we look at how a child compares to other children of the same age or grade level, and it usually involves standardized testing. I call my version keeping up with the Joneses, homeschool style.

Sometimes I think I spend too much time wondering if my kids are on track in all the right places. After all, who decides what the "right" places are? Still, I rationalize, it is OK to be focused on the basics. Knowing that math has never been my strong point, perhaps I worry about math more than the other subjects.

I had my first chance for a live comparison when Bella was a first grader.

"How old was your sister when you were born?" The question came from Bella's friend one Sunday afternoon on the way home from church.

My eyes were glued on the road, but my ears were trained on the seats behind me as my daughter's companion questioned my child. Would this cute little first grader calculate the age differences in our family without benefit of paper, pencils or fingers while younger children bickered in the back of the van? I knew my own daughter could not yet figure it out alone. Had I failed? Were we keeping pace with other children?

"We need to do subtraction," the friend advised. "How old is your sister now?" There was a long, convoluted math process whereby my daughter's friend eventually declared that my oldest daughter, then 18, had been 2 years of age when Bella was born just six years earlier. She was very matter of fact. My daughter agreed that this must be the right answer—she hadn't started subtraction yet—and the two of them moved on to another topic, oblivious to my sigh of relief. It was a small comparison study, but I liked learning that my kid was just as confused as anyone else her age.

# Buggy Science

Earwigs—or earbugs as my daughter calls them—creep me out. Finding two in the shower one morning was unbearable. Once the panic wore off, the opportunity to learn about entomology and human behavior was born.

Society might declare that males and females are basically the same, but I don't believe it. In an informal study conducted here at home, I have observed that my girls and I all have similar reactions to bugs. Brian and the boys react differently from us.

First, a definition. For the purposes of my not-so-scientific study, a bug was defined as either an actual insect or spider. This was not the place for discriminating between critters with eight legs and others with six. My research revealed that a girl's reaction to either creature was statistically the same.

The definition of bug also included dust bunnies, pieces of dirt which are shaped like bugs or any irregular paint splash or shadow that may look, even for a moment, like an insect, spider or other, unidentified creepy-crawly organism.

I have learned that if you deal calmly and rationally with a bug in the bathroom, you are likely to be a male. If you deal calmly and rationally with the female who just left the bathroom screaming, you may be a saint.

In the interest of scientific discovery, I offered my children an educational summer challenge. I wanted them to discover any useful function performed by earwigs. If I saw earwigs as beneficial, I might come to appreciate them. Did they, in fact, have a purpose in life?

The girls looked at me in disbelief. One son took up the challenge. I think he just wanted to earn the prize—a trip to the arcade, on me.

My son soon informed me that earwigs eat waste. He considered this a useful function, and I conceded that it sounded fairly beneficial. I just wished they did not consider my shower stall to be the Moonlight Café.

My budding scientist learned about male and female earwig behavior, and his eyes brightened as he informed me that earwigs have wings. I had never considered that earwigs might be able to launch themselves and come at me. I could listen no more. So much for science.

# In Pursuit of Fitness

Integrating physical fitness into our homeschool routine can be a challenge. We hope to expose our children to a variety of physical activities, and we hope to cultivate in them a love of fitness. We can't inspire them if we are sitting on the couch ourselves.

Over the years, our children have participated in various team sports, but seasons—and interests—come and go. We needed something more consistent. Early morning calisthenics were Brian's idea. I'd like morning a lot more if it just started later in the day, but I went along. After the stretches and other exercises, we ran.

I was passionate about running in my college days. Not particularly good at it, mind you, but determined. When I first took up running, I called up my friend Paige, and the two of us bundled up and set out on a three mile course through snow drifts. There was an indoor track at the university, but we had decided that was for sissies. Halfway through our run, Paige observed that our noses were running faster than we were. It was true, but we were undeterred.

In my 30s, I got serious and decided to run in the Sacramento Marathon. I would have made it, too, but a few weeks before the event, I broke my toe while putting on my shoe. Seriously. The toe was already weak from a previous break which occurred in a jazz dancing class. I'm not much of a dancer either.

By 40, I had given birth four times. None of my body parts had returned to the places God had put them originally. I became a fair weather runner.

I ran easily in my younger years, the miles on foot erasing my other excesses and rarely leading to more than a blister or stubbed toe. Now, with each step, I wonder if I will—like the running great, Jim Fixx—simply fall over and die.

My younger kids fight over the right to run along with me, and they eagerly participate in various other physical activities. I watch them develop agility, strength and confidence. They watch to see if I keep trying to get back in shape.

The first time I set out to keep up a consistent, postpartum running program, my oldest son took a break from working on the house to come along and encourage me. He was able to keep up while carrying an eight foot length of siding under one arm.

Through the years, I have not always been consistent as a runner, but I keep starting over, trying again. I often have a small group trailing behind me. At 4, Olivia complained that I was going "too fast." Nobody had ever accused me of that before. Now that the kids know I won't stop to talk and I am not likely to fall over, they often ride their bikes ahead, and I have a moment of painful solitude.

Have we been successful in teaching our children about fitness? I think so. They move for the joy of movement, not because they want to keep their cholesterol in check or lose a few pounds. If nothing else, my efforts should teach them about persistence. I keep moving now, slowly, with joints creaking and muscles screaming. I keep after my goal. I run now because my children are watching.

# Science at the Donut Shop

Getting out early in the morning is pretty tough for our family. At our house, getting everyone out the door in time for church on Sunday is nearly a miracle. One Sunday we surprised ourselves by being early. I loaded up the van and stopped at the donut shop.

It was a beautiful morning right up until the woman in front of me asked if I was out with my grandchildren. My pride wounded, we carted our selections to the van and headed to the park. As the kids munched their chosen sweets, I took the opportunity to start a science lesson.

"A scientist forms a hypothesis in order to prove something," I told the kids. They were sitting together, the empty pink donut box sitting between them. "Each of you was a scientist this morning."

The children munched their donuts and considered this statement. "How are we scientists?" one of them asked. It was exactly the opening I was waiting for.

"When we went to the donut shop this morning, each of you picked a donut you liked. Sophia picked an apple fritter. Max picked jelly-filled. Olivia and Bella picked cinnamon rolls. You all made your own hypothesis. That is like a guess. You wanted to have the best donut of all, so you guessed which one would be your favorite."

There was a brief discussion of the various merits of each type of donut. My hypothesis was confirmed: The most important factor in choosing a donut was size.

Textbook explanations of science offer up discussions of breeding pea plants for recessive traits and figuring out how to breed for desired characteristics. As scintillating a read as that may be, we like a more hands on approach. Donuts are definitely hands on.

"Now, in order to test your hypothesis, you need to taste other kinds of donuts," I told them. "If you really want to know which donut is the best, you would have to try every donut in the whole donut shop just to see for sure which you like the best. Then you would know for sure." Their eyes widened as they pondered the possibilities of trying every type of donut in the case.

Devoted now to the pursuit of scientific discovery, the kids started pinching off parts of their pastries. They began mixing, matching and sharing with siblings as I continued. "Now you are testing your hypothesis. When you try the other kinds, you make a decision about which donut you like the best."

Over the next few days, the kids came to me with various proposals for scientific exploration. "I've got a hypothesis," they'd say as each request was presented and considered. More gum would make them happy, fewer chores would have a similar effect. I felt a sense of satisfaction that the lesson had stuck. I could tell that future trips to the donut shop might lead to trying new things. Every day presents an opportunity to learn.

If you ever happen to see me in the donut shop early in the morning, understand that I'm only there to help my children with their research. Grab a fritter or a custard-filled donut and start an experiment of your own. Even science can be sweet.

# Driving Daze

"Dad's tires are illegal," my son informed me on our way home one day. I tried to imagine how my husband—as far as I knew, an honest guy—had come to be the owner of illegal tires. Had he brokered some black market deal? Taken on a life of crime?

His grandmother had hinted at a mafia connection when we'd visited in the '90s, but I thought she was making it up. With so many kids at home, I could not imagine how he found the time to assume the life of an outlaw. I needed clarification.

"How are Dad's tires illegal?"

"There isn't enough tread. But don't worry, the cops won't stop him for that."

My son was enrolled in driving school, and he had instantly become an expert in all things automotive.

I was thrilled to have somebody else talking to my child about the dangers of getting behind the wheel. The school had hours of scare-'em-straight videos. Nothing I could say compared with seeing blood on the big screen.

"Aren't you supposed to use a turn signal?" he asked on the way home.

We were on a country road with not a car in sight to see it blinking. I gritted my teeth and said nothing, but I flipped on my signal. He was watching, and my actions outweighed my words. Soon enough he would be behind the wheel, and I wanted him to follow all the rules when he got there.

The more I teach my kids, the more I learn. The one lesson any parent must know is this: The kids are watching. They see the example we set, they see our failures and shortcomings (and feel free to remind us of them). They see our triumphs.

Years ago my father taught me to drive an old beat-up Datsun pickup truck. While I didn't add any dents to the truck, I think I accounted for his heart condition.

I started out jerking along, trying to master the clutch. My father braced one hand on the dashboard and gripped the armrest with the other. Occasionally his eyes rolled back in his head and he screamed, "Get out of the ditch! Get out of the ditch!"

I was a little afraid of all those cars coming at me. He was afraid of all those trees coming at him.

Once I learned to stay on the road, my father passed along other advice: "Just because it's the speed limit doesn't mean you have to go that fast."

His favorite piece of wisdom has always been, "Look out for the other guy, 'cause he's not looking out for you."

My driving anxiety faded with time. Then my oldest son passed his written test, got his learner's permit, and I experienced the terror of learning to drive all over again. Now it was my turn to sit in the passenger seat and encourage without nagging. I found myself wanting to yell, "Get out of the ditch!" Mostly I kept quiet.

Fear does that to a person.

# Writing Kick

Somewhere around the middle of high school, Alyona went on a writing kick. Every chance she got, she sat at the computer, typing away. When she took a break she told me that the story was about a girl, orphaned under tragic circumstances. My daughter planned to write for a month and then be done. It was a monumental task. Occasionally she grabbed her dad or one of the younger kids to take a look.

I didn't get to read much, and I suspected that was my own fault. She was not looking for an editor, she wanted an admirer. What I think is creative correction, my daughter hears as criticism. Her creative muse is prolific but fragile.

Learning to keep my mouth shut is never an easy task. I am a grammar geek who thinks diagramming sentences is fun. Not that I've ever diagrammed a sentence in an effort to improve an essay. Not even all of my own sentences are complete.

After a summer of nearly non-stop reading, my daughter started using more punctuation in her writing. It certainly didn't come from any of those worksheets we argued over in earlier years. No, she punctuated when she was ready, and she was ready when she wanted to write something meaningful. Kids learn things when they want to know the answers.

She did not care about dangling participles or parallel structure. That may come in time (I can hardly wait!), but when the time came, she just wanted to write.

I was quite content to let my daughter spend long hours in front of the screen, transforming the pictures in her head into words.

I let her go, even as her writing took away time from other learning endeavors. I wanted her to develop her plots and refine her characters. This intensity did not last, but I believe she came away from her first bout of writing fever with a love of writing.

Having the ability to allow our children's interests to guide their learning has been one of the highlights of homeschooling. I have been able to shepherd them through the dry spells and to allow creativity in different areas. Sometimes I have been a coach, other times a cheerleader. Some days I have been a spectator on the sidelines, watching in amazement as my children learn.

My younger ones watched Alyona, and they wanted to write too. I started by having them draw pictures. Each picture had a story, I told them, and I would write down what they said. It did not matter if the stories made sense. I wrote them down. After a while, I asked them to copy what I had written. Soon enough they were asking to write the stories themselves. Apparently, I was too slow.

With their big sister writing an epic tale, the younger ones were discontent with mere pen and paper. They were itching to get their hands on a keyboard. I was tempted to make them endure typing lessons for the sake of efficiency. I thought about droning on about subjects, verbs and prepositional phrases.

Instead, I loaded paper into the printer and stood back. It was great to watch them learn.

# Diversity and Equality

If you wonder at all how we are qualified to homeschool our children, this should really clinch it for you: We don't even have a diversity training program. Brian and I just try to do a whole bunch of stuff with a whole bunch of people. There is no lesson plan, no state standard. Scandal, I know.

If we implemented a class in diversity training, we might spend more time worrying and wondering about all the dissimilarities and not so much time simply enjoying our friendships with people who are not carbon copies of us. We are probably scarred for life, and we are certainly damaging our children by not pointing out every difference we can find in the people around us.

Growing up in New York, my husband learned Italian and English at the knee of his great-grandmother. He spent a lot of time with his grandparents who, as they reminded him, "came over on da boat" and went through Ellis Island. His family worked on assimilating, and he never thought of himself as having a hyphenated ethnic designation. He has always been simply an American.

Some of our kids were born in Russia. Their culture and language from birth were very different than what they are now. Their heritage is part of who they are, but it is not all that they are. I tease my daughter that she is required by law to like beets, but she doesn't believe me. Apparently, some stereotypes aren't true. Maybe there is a lesson in that.

"We hold these truths to be self-evident, that all men are created equal," Brian began a discussion over dinner on the Fourth of July.

Sophia asked, "What does equal mean?" "Equal" is a math word, you see, and it didn't make sense that men would be part of an equation.

Sophia had been lobbying for a discussion of World War II, a topic that has fascinated her since we talked about it over dinner on the 60th anniversary of D-Day. Instead, she got a lesson on the Revolutionary War and the Declaration of Independence. This seemed acceptable, she just needed clarification of some key points.

Equality. How do you explain it to a child? Maybe if we could figure it out, we could explain it the media and our nation's lawmakers.

At the time, Sonia Sotomayor was making the rounds in Washington, preparing for hearings in which she was eventually confirmed as a Supreme Court Justice. When she was first nominated, the big news of the day was not about her performance on the bench or her personal and professional experience. No, her ethnic heritage made headlines. She is a Latina. No, maybe we should say she is Hispanic. Talk show hosts spent hours talking about which was the appropriate terminology.

I just gave up listening as the conversation moved to parsing out the ethnic and gender makeup of the Supremes through history. Never mind what Sotomayor is made of if she fits into the diversity mold. Is that equality?

Are all men created equal?

On June 25, 2009, two men died. One man lived his life in the public eye, rising to fame at a young age. He was repeatedly accused of unspeakable crimes against children while he was practically worshipped by millions. His funeral was a media circus with nonstop coverage.

The other man, Lt. Brian Bradshaw, lived his life anonymously. He fought to preserve the freedoms of this country, and he died, far from home, on the foreign soil of Afghanistan. His death might have gone completely unnoticed by the media if his aunt had not written a letter to the Washington Post. Even so, he did not get the adulation of millions of strangers, a televised funeral and celebrity tributes.

Next time we discuss current events over dinner, I'm hoping my kids don't ask why so much attention was paid to Michael Jackson while a brave warrior got barely a mention. Thinking about the inequality somehow makes me lose my appetite.

# Divas and Dancing Girls

I am a product of a public school system that had very little emphasis on the arts. I am not a musician, an artist, or a dancer. I just don't have it in my blood. When I was a child, my piano teacher politely suggested that I quit. My high school band teacher assigned me to play the crash cymbals. Occasionally she sent me to clean out the uniform closet. My college dance teacher said I was the only student she ever had who broke a toe in class.

Now I find myself a mother of children who want to learn to do things I never mastered. I want to be supportive. I want to help them learn, but sometimes my role as stage mother overwhelms me.

Take picture day for dance class, for example. My job was to take three squirmy girls, stuff them into ballet garb, coax their hair into buns, apply stage makeup and transport my ballerinas in pristine condition to the studio. I was a wreck.

Once you put a little girl in a tutu, she is unable to hold still. And getting bangs worked into a bun defies the laws of physics as we know them. We got to the studio ten minutes late. The girls were delighted, and they floated up the stairs, each step jarring another hair loose.

I didn't want my girls to know I was a rank amateur, so I found a girl with a perfect bun and asked her mom for help. "Don't worry," she told me as she whipped out a Samsonite case full of hair accessories. I was in the skilled hands of a professional.

My rescuer started with extra long bobby pins and told me the trick about unflavored gelatin and water as hair gel. It was too late for that solution, so another mom called out from the back, "I've got hair glue!" Hair glue? I didn't even know they made such a thing. She passed me the tube with surgical precision. I smoothed the hair glue on my daughter's locks and felt a calm settling over me.

When it came time to watch my little ballerinas dance on stage for the first time, their exuberance reminded me of the first time I watched my oldest daughter sing in concert. She stood on the bleachers, eyes closed, swaying back and forth in her blue choir robe. She wasn't supposed to be swaying, but I didn't know that. I saw the joy on her face, and I vowed then that we would do whatever we could to help our children develop a love for the arts.

Since then, I have attended concerts and operas, bought ads in programs, shuttled kids to lessons and glued unruly hair into place. I'm still more at home in my old blue sweatshirt than dressed up for a night at the symphony. But I'm learning.

# Thanksgiving Theater

Every mother dreams of the day when her child will star in the school play. When our kids set their own goals, we see a lot of theatrical productions. One Thanksgiving, history took on a whole new look.

Perhaps they were inspired by a night at the opera, possibly they just had enough free time to dream something up. Maybe I piled enough fabric scraps up that my daughter was inspired to sit and sew. I like to hope they were overtaken by an urge to explore history in a new way.

For days, there was a buzz around the house about the upcoming performance. The kids spent most of Thanksgiving working on final details. Alyona's sewing machine hummed along as she designed and put together costumes for the cast. All the participants swore themselves to secrecy in order to surprise us.

Squanto was the first to make an entrance. She—in this case, Squanto was a she—proceeded to make introductions: Captain John Smith, Princess Sacajawea (who insisted that her name was Sagajawea, most certainly NOT Sacajawea) and Queen Isabella. I made a mental note to brush up on history timelines.

At some point, the girls had written in a part for Farmer Jed since Max, then 2, insisted on wearing a cowboy hat and crashing practice time. By opening night,

Farmer Jed had lost interest. Instead, he grabbed a pair of his sister's pink ballet tights and put them on his head, the legs of the tights flopping like long pink ears. The Easter Bunny had crashed the Thanksgiving play.

As I looked around, I noted that the costumes looked strangely familiar. I caught glimpses of several of my old shirts in one configuration or another. My budding seamstress had a creative imagination.

Captain Smith, Princess Sagajawea, Queen Isabella and Squanto went through their lines as we all tried to ignore the Easter Bunny. That wasn't so easy to do, especially when he commandeered one of the seats at the Thanksgiving feast and pretended to eat the plastic strawberries.

The official play was followed by an interpretive dance performed by Princess Sagajawea and Squanto with another surprise addition by the Easter Bunny. I think he was doing some sort of ballet, but I'm not sure. Queen Isabella sat on the sidelines and offered him some advice: Don't pick your nose while you are dancing.

It all ended rather abruptly. The Easter Bunny tried to take over control of the sound system and got booted by Captain Smith. His howling woke the baby in the other room. Princess Sagajawea did her best to keep the show going by singing through "God Bless America" four times, but the momentum was gone.

When I mentioned that the historical connection was a bit fuzzy, Alyona reminded me that it is difficult to write a historically accurate script when two of the actors insist that they will only play royalty. There were other casting issues as well that led to this haphazard history fest.

I couldn't wait to see who showed up in the Christmas play.

# Youth Chorus

My high school band teacher never turned away a student. The summer before my senior year, I told her I wanted to play an instrument. She happened to have a bassoon lying around so she gave it to me, along with some sheet music, and sent me on my way. I think she secretly hoped I would give up and move on.

With the start of my senior year, I proved her half right. I'd given up the bassoon, but I had not moved on. I still wanted to be in the band, as long as it meant skipping first period. Mrs. Ingham assigned me to the percussion section and told me I could play the crash cymbals. Occasionally she would assign the triangle player and me a few special tasks like cleaning out the uniform room. Still, I am happy to report, our band made it to the state competition that year where we received the highest ranking possible. Nobody except the triangle player noticed when I fell asleep in the sight reading portion. At my graduation, Mrs. Ingham didn't exactly say she would miss me, but she did say nobody played the cymbals quite like I did.

That might have been the end of my musical education if a friend had not told us about a local youth chorus a few years ago.

At the first performance, my daughter closed her eyes, swayed back and forth in her blue robe, and sang. Oh, how she sang! I cried.

For the next few years, I wept through concerts, recitals, competitions and a couple of operas. Each time I was amazed at the music the voice teacher was able to coax from the young singers who participated. The level of training was first-rate.

Mrs. Johnson brought into our lives a rare quality. She could look at a child and not see someone who picked on her brother or dumped clean clothes into the hamper instead of putting them away. She looked at a child and saw potential. She called all of her students "my darling," and she made them believe they were. She was demanding, she was a perfectionist, she was talented, she was caring. Over the years, Mrs. Johnson proudly watched as her darlings went on to successful careers and hobbies in the choral arts. She can rattle off a list of former students who have taught and performed music locally and across the country.

The challenge of transforming squirmy children into performance artists is nothing when compared to the challenge of keeping a program afloat with declining enrollment and budget cuts. People always say there is nothing to do, but when it came time to support our local youth choir, too many folks were sitting at home.

We do our children a disservice if we teach them that entertainment comes only in the forms of television, movies and video games. Anyone can lament the loss of arts education in a community, but that complaint rings hollow when we, as a community, allow arts education to die. When we are not willing to pay a small amount so that our children can learn to expand their minds and voices, we are saying that we value arts education only if it is free.

Once our local choir folded for lack of participation, we started looking for a way to continue our children's musical education. Outside of marching band, my crash cymbal playing skill was fairly useless. I admire the talent of those who can play a more practical instrument. I want my children to be proficient in music, and the piano seemed a good place to start with lessons. Of course we outsourced.

We started with group lessons. I didn't even know one could take group piano lessons, but I am generally open to new things and, lacking even the most basic musical ability, I was willing to concede that group lessons might just work. Plus, it cut down on commuting.

The instructor invited me to attend the first lesson. I thought I heard her say there would be nine children and five pianos. When I arrived, I realized I had missed the part about the organ. I braced myself.

Out of the chaos came order. There were kinesthetic activities to engage active bodies, book work to help children get familiar with reading music, flashcards and more. While some of the children worked on activities, there was always a group at the pianos, playing.

I was a little stunned that first time, not sure what good might come of it. As time passed by, I came to be in awe of the procedure.

When I go to pick up the girls, I enjoy listening to the lessons. The instructor's voice rings out above the cacophony, "C! A minor! F!" she coaxes as she plays along. It is all meaningless to me. Apparently it is meaningless to some of the students as well. She stops the music often to offer individual instructions as needed then starts again, calling out directions as she goes. "C, Sophia, that's a C," she says, and I wonder how she can tell who is off.

Like all good piano teachers, ours schedules recitals. It is an opportunity for the children to showcase their talents to an eager audience. Some people, though, should not attend piano recitals. Those people are called 2-year-olds. I guess I wasn't thinking clearly—having a house full of kids will do that to a mother—and I brought mine along. She did great for the first 30 minutes when everyone was getting settled. The start of the recital was, however, the end of her cooperation.

"Mommy, butt!" she announced in between songs. I thought that might be the end of it, so I decided to stay and hear my kids. Fortunately, they were all at the beginning of the recital. That still wasn't early enough to stop the noise from my little one.

The speech pathologist in me wanted to point out that using two words together is a developmental milestone that usually takes place by a child's second birthday. I could have discussed how Sicily's extensive vocabulary, use of synonyms for the word "butt," and emerging short sentences demonstrated that her language development was coming along well. The mom in me wanted to slide under the chair. As soon as possible, we slipped outside where we sat on a chair and listened from afar. Sicily proudly continued naming body parts.

A few weeks later, we were listening to classical music on the car radio. Olivia announced, "That's Handel. I didn't play Handel at the recital. I only played Grieg." I didn't even know there was a Grieg. Apparently, he didn't write much for the crash cymbals.

# Gas Prices Lead to Economics Lesson

I spent an entire Sunday evening trying to explain the principles of supply and demand to a 6-year-old. By the time the conversation was over, I think I learned something from her, but it wasn't about economics.

The impromptu lesson started after a family discussion. When gas prices topped four dollars a gallon, we talked about how it was taking an extra 20 dollars to fill the gas tank compared to how much it cost us just a week earlier. Brian told the girls, "Nobody gives us an extra 20 dollars, we just have to save money in other places so we can buy gas to take you places." We reminded the kids of some of the changes we had made to our family budget. Reducing allowances was one of our financial trade-offs.

A few hours later, Sophia met me at the computer. "Mommy, why does it cost more for gas this week?" she asked.

"Well, the price just got more expensive," I stalled. I was supposed to be writing. I didn't think I had time to talk. She thought I did.

"Why would the people who sell the gas make it more expensive?"

I began to suspect that this conversation was not going away. I had not considered teaching this child economics in our homeschool because I was pretty sure we had planned to wait past the tail end of kindergarten.

I picked up a doll from the floor. That poor doll had been drawn on, had her hair cut and she was lying on the floor in all her naked glory, waiting for this teachable moment. "OK," I began, "imagine that you want to sell this dolly. Do you think anyone would buy this dolly?"

Sophia giggled and stuck her tongue through the gap where her teeth were just starting to grow back in. I took that to mean yes.

"So let's say Bella wants to buy this dolly for a dollar. Would you sell this dolly to Bella for only one dollar?"

"Sure," she replied.

"But what if a whole bunch of people started knocking on the door and they all wanted to buy this dolly, and one person wanted to buy this dolly for three dollars. Would you still sell the dolly to Bella for only one dollar?"

"Well, if she really wanted the dolly, I would give it to her." She grinned at me, confident she had given the right answer.

I hugged her tight and wished she ran an oil company. Then I started over. I explained that everyone uses gas, and sometimes, when everyone wants something, it starts to cost more because everyone is buying it. I wasn't sure if she understood or if she was just finished with the conversation. Once we got past the dolly part, her eyes kind of glazed over.

She left, and I returned to writing.

A few minutes later, my daughter bounced back into the room. She bounces everywhere, this one.

"Mom, I have something for you," she said. She thrust her hand at me, insisting that I stop and pay attention to her. In her hand, she held two crumpled dollar bills.

"This week," she told me, "you get an allowance from me." She hugged me and skipped back out, leaving me, as she often does, in awe.

# Part Three

# Socialization

The lack of emotional security of our American young people is due, I believe, to their isolation from the larger family unit. No two people - no mere father and mother - as I have often said, are enough to provide emotional security for a child. He needs to feel himself one in a world of kinfolk, persons of variety in age and temperament, and yet allied to himself by an indissoluble bond which he cannot break if he could, for nature has welded him into it before he was born.
~Pearl S. Buck

# The "S" Word

No matter how many times I hear the "S" question, I am astounded by it. I am never quite sure what it means. I hear the words, and I understand them all, it is just the collective whole that I find puzzling. Of all the questions I hear about homeschooling, one comes up more often than any other.

"What about socialization?"

There, I've done it. The socialization question is out there.

I never seem to know what a person is asking. Is the person asking if our children ever leave the house? If we spend time with others? I am rarely asked about academics. Could it be that other people's children hop off to traditional schools solely to spend time on the playground?

Secretly I hope that I am being asked if I ever get to socialize. Maybe I'm being asked out for some kid-free, adult conversation at a coffee shop. I think I recall that kind of socialization. We all drink out of big girl cups, and nobody uses the word "potty" in a sentence. Oh, yes, I remember.

Reality strikes: Nobody is asking about me. Ironically, we are often in a social situation when the conversation begins.

I want to point out to them that socialization is not—or should not be—about succeeding in a room full of same-aged peers. Socialization at its best should be about developing social skills with people of all ages.

Regular socialization with all age groups reduces the peer pressure and the crushing need for conformity so many children feel. Expecting a child to benefit from social skills modeled only by children is setting them up for failure.

Instead of arguing, it is easier to play along and answer the question. I have a standard litany memorized listing all social activities in which my children participate, from music lessons to church activities to volunteer work to play dates with friends. After my list, the next question is often, "How do you keep up with it all?"

To say that homeschooling happens only at home is like saying that a stay-at-home mom doesn't work. Homeschooling takes place in the bank, in the post office, in the grocery store and just about anywhere a family goes. Each of those places provides a realistic opportunity for socialization.

My children—and your children, if you take them places and expect them to learn how to participate in society—are exposed to a variety of people each week. They interact with people in all age groups and learn to adjust their communication styles to fit each unique situation.

Every community interaction provides an opportunity for adults to model appropriate behavior. The voices our children hear are shaping their development. When the clerk at the store takes a moment to help my daughter count out her change, my daughter learns more than simple math skills, she learns about customer service. When a local beekeeper shows my children how he harvests honey, my kids get a sweet lesson in science.

In between scheduled socialization, the kids skip off to build forts, play ponies, ride bikes, or host a sleepover. They call it playing with friends. I call it a chance to slip out for a cup of coffee.

# The Pig in the Pantry

For four years, we kept a pickled pig in the pantry. By the time the pig came in the mail, I'd forgotten I'd ordered it, consumed as I was with morning sickness. I shoved the vacuum-packed bag behind some books and forgot about it.

The pig took turns in my sons' closet, on the shelf in the pantry and, occasionally, in our school room. Meanwhile, I went through morning sickness, pregnancy and the chaos that a new baby brings. Three times.

Occasionally my son would wander in and ask "Mom, are we ever going to do anything with that pig?"

"Yeah," I'd say, "move it to the shelf." It was never the answer he was looking for, but it managed to get the pig out of the way for a while. But sooner or later, the pig was going to have to be dealt with.

One day I snapped. In a burst of inspiration and bravado, I invited five other homeschool families over for Science Daze. The pig was having a coming out party.

Making invitations was easy, and I started looking forward to finally dissecting a pig with the kids. Calmly, I assured the other mothers it would be fun. As the day drew near, I did what any rational mother of seven would do. I asked Brian to stay home from work and deal with the pig.

On the appointed day, the families began arriving. Kids burst in from everywhere, all asking "When are we cutting open the pig?" We had 22 children in the house and three hours until the big event.

Each of my older children had chosen a science experiment to teach their guests. After dividing into groups, the visiting children rotated through the four stations. For convenience, children were divided along age lines so that each presentation could be geared up or down according to the audience. The experiments included electricity, the moon, flight and gravity.

By having the older kids teach the younger ones, all the adults enjoyed a few moments together by the fire comparing homeschool notes.

After lunch and a time of running around outside, the kids were ready for the main attraction. With a booming voice and much fanfare, my husband introduced the pig. The kids huddled around, pushed, shoved and strained for a better view. The scent of formaldehyde wafted through the house, prompting one mother to go for a long walk.

Brian patiently explained the digestive and respiratory systems as children and adults peered in. Nobody could tell he was drawing upon his own high school biology days, and not upon the instructions that had come with the pig. They'd been lost for years, a fact that caused a slight panic on the morning of the event. An Internet search yielded instructions for a frog, but no pig, so he was on his own, mumbling in my general direction about getting roped into such things. I'm sure I have no idea what he meant.

The younger ones wandered in and out, but about half the kids stuck with it for two hours. When it was done, there wasn't much left of the pig.

As families packed up and started for home, my 3-year-old rushed in the house, caught her breath and asked, "Now can we cut open the frog?"

"Yeah, baby," I said, "just as soon as Mommy finds him." I'm sure he's around here somewhere.

# Impress Your Friends—Play Waste Bingo

It was my daughter's sixth birthday. Finally freed from the cruel injustice of sitting in a booster seat, Bella was begging to hit the road. The destination was not as important as the journey itself, so we decided to take in the recycling, grab a mocha and pick up a cheesecake. The day had promise.

Once at the recycling center, Bella helped me sort through bags of assorted bottles and cans. She meticulously removed lids from plastic bottles and separated glass, aluminum and plastic into their designated bins.

We took our bounty and headed to the restroom to wash up. On the way out, we stopped to look at bales of crushed cans as she wondered aloud what anyone could do with so many cans.

More than a year went by before I got up the nerve to call and ask for a tour. I thought the lady who answered the phone might find my request a bit odd, but she said she enjoys guiding hundreds of kids through the facility each year. She invited us to come on out. We set up a field trip

59

to go learn what goes on at the dump, and we invited a bunch of homeschooling friends.

By now, most of our friends think we are a little bit conked in the head. This was the clincher. We only had one family decide to come along with us, and I suspected it was because they were new in town.

We arrived at the appointed time and learned that we were not visiting the dump. We were visiting the transfer station. For years, I had given directions to my house that included the phrase, "Go out of town, past the dump." Transfer station sounded a little classier, so I did my best to sound hip after that.

We all donned bright vests and took off on a walking tour. The grounds were remarkably clean, considering all that goes on there. We got to see old trash toters being baled up to be recycled, trucks coming and going and some of the sorting that goes on to separate recyclables from other trash that goes out of the facility and to the landfill.

The kids learned a lot about recycling that day, and they kept an eye on us to remind us to do our part. One change we made as a family was to reduce the number of plastic bags we used. Brian switched to paper on his weekly grocery trip, and the kids estimated that we would avoid using over 600 plastic bags in a year just by making that switch. Next we accumulated a stash of reusable cloth bags to use for some of our other shopping trips.

As we stood on the truck scale, we added another bit of math into the trip. The kids calculated that our combined weight was just under a half ton. The adults jumped off before the little mathematicians could start figuring further.

Our trip ended with a box of loot. Our tour guide handed out a couple of games of Waste Bingo, and some mini recycling toters that the kids used as banks.

Back at the house, we washed up and I made a snack for all. I was going to make dump cake, but after learning the proper terminology I couldn't figure out how to make transfer station cake. We settled on cupcakes.

# Ticket

I remember a television show from my childhood days called "Let's Make a Deal." Monte Hall, the host of the show, would periodically leave the stage to walk into the audience. He would pick an audience member and offer a prize if that person could produce a specific item. Women would rummage through their purses furiously, and the crowd would cheer. I used to imagine what might happen to me if I somehow made it onto the show.

Since my children had never seen that show, I provided them with a homeschooler-meets-community version. Sitting in my van on the side of the road, a stranger asked if I had a couple items of interest to him. Let me tell you what I found. The console drawer yielded a box of heartworm pills for the dog, a calculator, a coffee cup, assorted receipts and one cookie cutter. Between the seats I had a copy machine and a pair of jumper cables.

I might have won the prize if I had been stopped by Officer Monte Hall. Alas, he was not the one asking me to find the prize in this game. A police officer with no sense of humor wanted to know if I had my registration and proof of insurance. Sadly, I did not.

There was also that little question about my rate of speed. The officer had reason to believe that I might have exceeded the limit by a wee bit. Now, it may be true that I have, on rare occasion, regarded the signs along the side of the road as mere suggestions, but in general, I follow the rules. The place where I was pulled over is generally not an area I'd risk our safety by exceeding the limit.

Except on that day. While my eyes focused on the road, my brain was tossing around so many things. Could the girls plan a sleepover? How many apple trees should I plant this year? Should I buy a new cow or wait a couple months until the pasture was flush with grass? And in my distraction, I sailed along with traffic and didn't notice how fast we were going.

It only got worse. Because I could not find my registration and proof of insurance, there was even more to explain, both to the officer and to my children.

There were benefits to the traffic stop. Max, age 5 at the time, was insulted that he still had to be constrained by a car seat when he was so nearly an adult. When the officer checked out the interior, it meant reinforcement of the rule. For myself, it was a reminder. Nothing is more important than keeping my kids safe. The trivialities of life—however frustrating or distracting—can wait.

# The Class We Didn't Want to Take

The first phone call was routine enough. An employee called in sick at our family business. I checked with the rest of the staff to make sure everything was covered and didn't think too much about it. Distractions of home occupied my thoughts until the phone rang the next morning. Roberta would be out again, probably for the rest of the week. "No problem," I told her husband. "We've got it covered. Tell her to get some rest."

When the third call came, I was expecting a routine update. "We're taking Roberta to the hospital," her husband said. "She has pneumonia."

"Some people will do anything to get out of work," I joked. We talked for a bit and hung up. Everything would be back to normal soon.

Except it wouldn't.

Brian answered the fourth call. I was outside when he came with the news that Roberta had passed away.

I wandered back into the house with tears streaming down my face. Max was on the step stool at the kitchen sink. At 5, he loved washing dishes, and we had plenty of opportunity for him to practice. Max looked at me, tilted his head and asked what was wrong.

"Miss Roberta died," I told him, "and even though I know I'll see her again in heaven, I'm sad because I miss her now."

"Don't worry, Mom," he said, "you'll see her again soon. You're old."

If that kid ever does find someone to marry him, she better not ask if her new dress makes her look fat. He will say yes.

Thus comforted by my son, I went to tell the girls. I can't say it sunk in for any of us until later. For me, it hit me hardest when I went into the office.

I guess you'd say she was a receptionist, but Roberta was a friend first. People say you should never hire friends to work for you. If there is a problem, you might not feel comfortable talking it through they say. It is probably true because I'm sure I drove her crazy, and she never mentioned it at all.

The next day at the office, I half expected to see Roberta sitting at the desk. She would tell her stories and ask about the kids. Roberta loved kids, and it showed. Many times, she rocked a baby in one hand and did the filing with the other. My kids grew up taking her hugs for granted.

Talk of "Miss Roberta" came up periodically as the children started to process the loss of a friend. A few weeks later, the younger girls danced in a ballet recital that was dedicated to Roberta's memory. Heading home, Max started sobbing as he climbed into his booster seat and put on his seat belt. "Miss Roberta is dead!" he yelled as the tears flowed. "I miss her, and it's not fair!"

We talked about it again, picked up some ice cream to celebrate the recital and soothe the hurts, and went home.

There is much to learn, even in sorrow, even when we don't want the opportunity. Grief is a class I didn't want to take, didn't want to teach to my children.

Roberta requested that we celebrate her life rather than mourn her death. The kids helped me to bake cookies to take along to the memorial service. There were stories and hugs all around. Roberta was a hugger. There was laughter mixed with tears, a bittersweet ending to a life well-lived.

# Christmas Visit

Whenever I make popcorn, I remember time spent with an old friend. I first met her back when I was a child. She taught Sunday school, and every now and then she rounded up a bunch of the children to go visit "old people." The irony was, even then Mrs. Hodges was the oldest person I knew.

I was a pretty shy kid, and I worried a lot about those trips to convalescent hospitals. I remember that we sang a few songs, but the rest was a blur. From my vantage point in the back corner, the golden years didn't glitter much. I never could escape having my cheeks pinched. I knew it was important to go, I just wished someone else would take my place.

Somewhere between when I finished college and started graduate school, Mrs. Hodges pretended she needed help, just about the time I needed a place to stay. On Sunday evenings, she would make popcorn and lemonade and then dish up some chocolate chip ice milk. I spent a year there, getting my head on straight and soaking up her warmth. Right about the time I was able to support myself, my friend recovered enough that she could live alone again. Some coincidence.

From time to time I remembered her example and thought of taking the kids to visit lonely folks in skilled nursing facilities, but I was always reluctant to start. Again, there is irony. In my work as a speech pathologist, I have worked with all ages, but I prefer working with the geriatric population. I go to facilities in a professional capacity and feel perfectly comfortable interacting with the residents. I have just worried that my children would be nervous, and I let that be an excuse for complacency.

One winter, we flew to New York and took the kids to meet their great-grandmother who lived in an assisted living facility. I was uncertain as to how my children would react to a room full of strangers in wheelchairs. I realized that all that time I had put off such a visit thinking the kids would have the same trepidation I'd once had. I was completely mistaken.

We entered while the residents were involved in an activity. Without hesitation, the kids joined in a game of balloon volleyball. We watched the residents perk up. They smiled, they talked, they hugged. And yes, they pinched cheeks. My kids didn't seem to mind. In fact, all this attention only encouraged them to ham it up some more. We were all sorry to leave.

Once we got home, I decided that it would be good for all of us to go visit a local facility and bring some Christmas cheer. Brian and I sat down with the kids, not sure what they would think of my plan. Instead of complaining, they started making out a caroling list and planning time to write out cards to lonely folks who might not have any visitors that Christmas.

We spent Christmas that year with strangers in an Alzheimer's unit. We knew they were not likely to remember us after we left, but I hoped the children would remember the importance of visiting.

# Lessons Learned on Sunday

Homeschool families are often portrayed as close-knit families with well-behaved children. Such stories sustain me through the times when things don't go so well, for days when just making it through the day is the biggest goal I can muster. Our family stands out. We have a lot of kids, we homeschool and we like to go places.

I used to be on time, but those days are long gone, a mere remnant of a life when I thought that if mothers tried harder, their children would sit up straight and behave themselves. Now I know better.

Still, I am eternally optimistic that we can slip into church on time. One special Sunday, I coaxed my children out of bed, plied them with pastries and loaded them into the van. It was tight, but I was hoping to make it to church on time. Brian and Alyona had gone in early—he to volunteer, she to be part of a performance group. I had only five little ones to get ready that day.

We straggled in a few minutes late, and I prayed that the families around me would understand. Just as the usher found us a spot to sit together, a violinist began a solo. For one brief moment, all was as it should be. This, I remembered, was how it felt to sit in church.

Then the ushers began passing the offering bags, and my son decided to participate. Max, then 2 years old, nearly came to blows with his sister over who would be the helper. I turned to see the couple behind me shaking with laughter as the violinist solemnly played on.

The man sitting on the other side of us had either missed the action or loved a good brawl. When the registration book passed by, he started to pass it to Max, only to have the woman behind us nearly leap over the pew to rescue the book from my son's hands.

Suddenly the lights dimmed, and the on-stage performance began. I sat next to five children whose eyes were fixed on the stage, watching their big sister. I started to relax. Maybe we would make it through. I looked around. Nobody was looking at us anymore.

When the performance was finished, the pastor began a prayer. This has always been the hardest time for my little ones. Max often wanted to add his own commentary. This time, my son was looking for clues. He looked around, then bowed his head. He looked up, then closed his eyes again. Look, close, look, close, look, close.

At that moment, I had a couple of realizations. First, the smell that was permeating the air was coming from the baby. Second, I had forgotten the diaper bag, and the contents of the current diaper were slowly seeping through his clothes and mine.

The pastor kept praying. I said a prayer of my own.

After only 10 minutes, I was headed for the door with all five children in tow. I hoped to keep a low profile as the pastor began the sermon, but Olivia had gotten herself dressed that day, and she picked shoes that were pretty. Didn't fit her, but they were pretty. As we snuck out of the sanctuary, everyone could hear a low wail, "But Mommy, my shoe fell off!"

People often tell me they are praying for me. Now you know why.

# French Fries, Limousines and the Voices of Experience

"I'm not ordering French fries," my son proclaimed as we made a rare visit to a drive-thru. "They're just soaked in oil." For a moment, I was filled with pride as I wondered if my son had learned from my fine example of dietary restraint or if he really had been listening to my rantings on the benefits of proper nutrition. I was so absorbed with congratulating myself that I almost missed his next statement: "Yeah. Mrs. Rex told me about it."

So much for learning at home. The conversation served as a reminder, too, of the importance of community. Our kids are out there in the world, listening to many voices. I'm glad that, on this one day, the voice my son heard had a message I agreed with.

A few years back, I read about creating a ceremony to mark the transition from childhood to adulthood. The idea bounced around in my head until it gelled into a plan.

Ordinarily, our family birthday celebrations are pretty low key. We try to instill in our children that there are more important things in the world than piles of presents. Turning 14 is a time for a little extra something.

"Mom, there's a limo outside." Alyona's voice had just a touch of reverence. Limos are cool. When the driver walked through the door a few minutes later, she didn't make the connection. We were at my office, and people came in to see me all the time. This time, someone was coming to see her.

We didn't have anywhere in particular that we needed to go. We picked up a friend, made a few stops, reveled in the cool factor, and went to dinner. Once we got back to the office, the celebration started.

My daughter had been allowed to invite two friends, but other than that, the room was filled with women who had played an important role in our lives as mentors and friends.

Soon after we began, I told my daughter's story. I described how we traveled to the other side of the world to find her and how we gave her the middle name of Faith because everything about her adoption required just that. My eyes filled with tears as I realized how close I'd come to not ever knowing this remarkable young lady.

The most important piece of the evening was the reading of the letters each woman had prepared. Many spoke of the angst of the teenage years and the hope of the future. I watched as my daughter took it all in.

My rather reserved daughter talked all the way home. She marveled at each gift she had received, commented on each letter. I don't know how many times she thanked me for the evening. She said it was the best night of her life. Once we got home, she gave a detailed account to her father and a younger sister who had managed to wait up. Alyona remembered to write thank you notes without any reminders.

In years to come, she will draw on the counsel she heard on this evening and in everyday life. My daughter may not always listen to my voice, but I hope she will remember her special day and seek out those voices that inspire her to be the kind of young woman we believe she has the potential to become. In other words, I can always depend on Mrs. Rex.

# Learning on the Road

When we travel, we prefer to take short trips during the school year when roads and destinations are not so crowded. For the most part we stay close to home. There is more time to explore if we don't spend so much time driving.

Occasionally, we get requests to go to Winnemucca, not that any of the little ones making the request can tell, with any degree of certainty, where that might be or why they would want to go there. It is a destination, and adventure is in their blood.

As with much of what we do, I wonder who is getting the most knowledge out of our field trips. Brian and I have learned many lessons about taking the family on the road, and I would like to pass along some of the wisdom gained over the years.

Many seasoned travelers will give you advice on how to pack efficiently, how to pick the best place to stay, or even where to go. I can tell you how to make your journey with your sanity more or less intact.

Travel experts recommend playing games to make the time pass more quickly. To those of you traveling with children, I offer this advice: Don't start out with the Hokey Pokey. It never ends.

When planning to take kids on a trip, remember that the cost of food is negotiable. The price of admission need not break the bank. A puke-free car is priceless.

Brian has always been one to enjoy an adventure. Before the kids came along, we'd head off to speech pathology conventions, and Brian would seek out the most interesting spots and meet me at the end of the day to function as tour guide. Now, with a van full of kids, his explorations are somewhat more focused on education.

Educators talk about teachable moments, those times in life where you grab an opportunity to teach a child about a subject as it comes up unexpectedly, perhaps a subject that might not otherwise be a part of the curriculum.

I have a homeschooling friend who confided that she once stopped her car to examine an owl that had been hit by the car in front of her. She and her children took a few moments to study this magnificent creature creating a memory that will stick better than any pencil-and-paper anatomy lesson. So far, we've not encountered any fresh road kill on our travels, and for that I am grateful. Brian would probably be game for the stop. He's more daring than I am.

It is fortunate that Brian came equipped with a booming voice because we drive a 15-passenger van. In order to communicate from one end to the other, we turn down the music and yell, a kind of redneck intercom system. "Look kids," he will begin, gesturing toward a sight along the way. This is where it gets tricky. Kids hear things that we don't say..

I personally have given up on pointing out landmarks and interesting scenery. I made the mistake of telling our girls we were crossing the San Mateo Bridge on a trip to the coast once. Since then, any road trip invites incessant questions about when we will cross the "Potato Bridge."

Brian believes in telling the truth. The poor man spent 10 minutes trying to explain that the Potato Bridge does not exist. He still imagines that he can change the minds of our children, but on this one, he finally gave up. He now refers to any structure spanning an expanse of water as the Potato Bridge. Trips just go easier that way.

My next piece of advice is to never, under any circumstances, take any exit without a full and detailed explanation of where you are going and why. Any time we exit, our kids ask if we are lost, and they are never shy to offer up helpful instructions.

As we pulled off the freeway to search for coffee on one of our day trips, a voice from the back wafted forward. "Dad! I think we're lost. You should go straight." Never take driving instruction from a 5-year-old. You may end up in Winnemucca.

Back on the freeway, Sophia commanded us to turn down the radio. "OK, Dad, you're going the right way now." She then proceeded to check in every so often to ask if we knew where we were going.

One other piece of advice. If you happen to drive on the Potato Bridge on your way to Winnemucca, and you get pulled over for driving a wee bit over the speed limit, tell the officer the truth. The kids are watching, and they remember everything.

# The Nine States of America

"Oh, MOM!" she squealed. "These are perfect! I'm gonna get these for Dad!" I turned to see my 5-year-old daughter holding a pair of boxers with a bold flag motif. One side sported a blue background with white stars, the other side was emblazoned with red and white stripes. I tried to imagine Brian's face when he opened this gift.

My job was supposed to be to come along and guide my daughter's choice of gifts for Father's Day. Just as I was turning to point out some sensible black socks, she found the boxers, and she made her decision.

"This is what Dad needs for the Nine States of America," she continued.

"The what?"

"The Nine States of America," she explained. "You know, our trip."

Then it hit me. We had been talking about taking a cross-country family trip. What we called the United States of America, Bella had heard as the "Nine States of America." She had caught my dream.

When I was a kid, we drove from California to Oklahoma to visit family almost every summer. After we moved back to Oklahoma, we drove out to California almost every summer to visit friends. Most years we stopped at the Grand Canyon and a few other sites—for about 15 minutes.

My father would have stopped at every historical marker along the road if we would have let him. One year we spent three hours looking for Sacajawea's gravesite. Found it, too. We stayed 15 minutes, took pictures, and moved on.

I may have grumbled here and there, but a part of me loved the journey.

Then several years ago, we hosted an exchange student from Brazil. Paula knew about a Rotary Club in Texas that organized a trip for exchange students every summer. She signed up and came back with 10 rolls of film. Paula had seen parts of America I had never heard of. My dream was born. We would see it all, too. I just had to convince the family.

After many years of contemplation, we picked a date and started some planning, only to find that the trip would have to wait another year. I swallowed my disappointment and kept adding to my travel file folder.

Then, by accident, I came across some information about Godfrey, Illinois, a town founded by a man with eight kids. I could see the photo—all of us standing in front of the sign that said "Welcome to Godfrey." We had to go. It didn't take much to convince Brian, and the kids thought that visiting the town of Godfrey, locally famous for an annual corn maze, might be worth the trip.

And so we set off on a cross-country journey. We planned to visit friends along the way, stop at historical markers and take photos of the highlights. It was just me, one big van, eight kids and Brian in his red, white and blue boxers.

# All Roads Lead to Godfrey

"Dad, we're late." Ed's voice echoed from the back of our 15-passenger van. We had a schedule to keep, he reminded us, and we were not going to make it.

We thought we'd planned every detail of our trip. Somehow, we forgot about time zones. We were going to be precisely one hour late to our hotel.

"We're on California time," Brian growled from the front.

"I knew you shouldn't have told them the time changed." I couldn't resist blaming this one on Brian. I would have kept quiet and reset all the watches during the night, but no, he wanted full disclosure. We tried to pacify them with an extra episode of Mythbusters on DVD, but Ed reminded us it wasn't on the schedule either.

We covered 10 states in our 17-day trip. Most days, the kids weren't as interested in the scenery as they were in the DVD of the day. In western Colorado, this was a tragedy. The mountains were breathtaking. About 10 minutes east of Denver I started to wish I could see the screen myself.

We stopped in out-of-the-way places—towns so small that the Wal-Mart trucks don't even slow down as they breeze by the exits on the interstate. One of those towns was Stratton, Colorado, near the Kansas border. The exit sign has an arrow pointing to the business district, a gross overstatement. With Ed keeping an eye on the time, we determined that it took all of three minutes to drive slowly down the main street and back again.

My laptop died in Stratton, and we decided to find a replacement the next day. We drove into Kansas, popped The Wizard of Oz into the DVD player, and Brian drove through tornado warnings as we searched for a place to buy a computer.

One of the kids piped up from the back, "Do they sell laptops in Kansas?"

We looked at each other with that knowing look parents get when their children have said something cute. "Now, kids, Kansas is not a third world country. We are still in the United States, you know."

After checking three mega stores, we had to revise Dorothy's wise observation: We were not in California anymore.

That observation served us well as we ventured into Missouri later in the trip. There we bought a new laptop and found grocery stores that served fried chicken gizzards as standard fare in the take out case. We couldn't get any takers from our crowd.

Our turnaround spot was Godfrey, Illinois, a town selected simply because it shared our last name. And they have a corn maze. Before we left, we told the kids we'd be taking a family picture in front of the town's welcome sign. If I was going to travel 5,124 miles in a van full of kids, I was going to have a picture for the Christmas card. I think they prayed all the way there that Godfrey wouldn't have a welcome sign. Turns out there were three signs, all located on main thoroughfares. There was no way to do this discreetly.

Tumbling out of the van on a blustery day, Katia was the first to be optimistic. "At least nobody we know will see us," she said. I guess I forgot to mention I was using that new laptop to write an article about the trip. Oops.

One afternoon, hurtling down the highway on our way towards home, a moment of calm overtook us. We had made pit stops along the way to refuel and rotate seat positions. We had arbitrated arguments, sung silly songs, played travel games and determined that no, we were not there yet. As the miles rolled by, we settled in to a quiet resolve. My thoughts turned toward catching up on my reading. Brian's thoughts turned to our lives.

"We made the right choice, you know."

I tried to clear my head and return to the present.

"We made the right choice," he repeated.

"About what?"

"This," he said, waving his hand toward the back of the van. "All of this."

"This trip?"

"No, not the trip. All of it."

I was still confused.

"We could have been driving that," he said, pointing to a sleek silver speedster that had slipped past us in the fast lane.

I tried to imagine all of us scrunched up in the back of a convertible. In my dreams, I drive a Miata. Red, of course. I tell the kids that if I ever get one, I'm taking out the passenger seat so nobody will fight over who gets to go with me.

"I don't think we would have fit into a sports car," I reminded him.

"No, probably not, but if we didn't have kids, we could afford a BMW or a Mercedes." I imagined the quiet ride, the smooth leather seats, the stereo system.

I looked in the mirror at our packed van with the row of car seats, containers of toys, and children still sticky from our last snack stop. The little ones had finally passed out. The older ones were reading, playing games and, at least for the moment, keeping their hands to themselves.

He was right. We made the right choice.

# Part Four

# Food

One of the very nicest things about life is the way we must regularly stop whatever it is we are doing and devote our attention to eating.
~Luciano Pavarotti

Food is the medium by which we nurture one another. Sadly, time spent together over a meal is no longer a daily occurrence in most families.

Increasingly, public schools are happy to add feeding the nation's children to their list of responsibilities. Between the breakfast program, the lunch program, after school snacks and the summer nutrition program, parents can, if they wish, allow the state to nourish their child's stomach as well as their child's mind. If we are not careful, we will have a generation of people who don't know how to cook real ingredients into real meals that provide real nourishment. Why would they need to when the government provides three squares a day?

As for the evening meal, the family dinner that used to be a part of American society has largely fallen by the wayside in favor of careers, activities and screen time. People strive to save every minute and every penny in order to rush home to heavily-mortgaged houses, heat up microwave dinners and use what was saved to pay for more channels than anyone can watch. The time for a family dinner is spent in front of a computer screen, communicating via social networking sites with people they don't care enough about to invite over for a real dinner.

Not on my watch. We cook. We eat. We learn.

# Marshmallows for Breakfast

Many years ago, Walter Mischel conducted a famous study at Stanford University. He gave a group of hungry 4-year-olds a marshmallow and a promise. If they could wait until he returned, they would get one more marshmallow. Some kids waited, others devoured the marshmallow they had and missed out on a second helping.

Fourteen years later, Mischel revisited the children and made some interesting observations. The children who had waited were judged to be more competent socially, more trustworthy and more successful. Those who waited even earned significantly higher SAT scores than the children who had been unable to delay gratification.

While I will admit to giving my kids marshmallows for breakfast, it is always with the disclaimer that it only happened once, and it was only because we didn't have any cheese puffs.

Let's face it—all those Christmas cards wishing peace on earth were really talking about the time of year when the kids go back to school after break. For homeschoolers, there are days when packing a lunch and waving good-bye sounds awfully tempting.

I had a theory that I could have a few moments of quiet if I gave the kids something to gum up their little mouths. I was right, but the peace didn't last long. Soon they were yelling for more, and I was joining them for a good half hour of sticky fun.

We discovered that it can be quite challenging to build a structure from a bag of miniature marshmallows and a box of toothpicks.

My husband reminds me that balance isn't only about cutting out the bad stuff, it is also about including the good stuff. And in the life of a child, marshmallows are definitely in the "good stuff" category.

The marshmallow and toothpick trick is an unstructured way to put some basic engineering lessons in front of the kids. Each time we try it, the race is on to see who can construct the tallest structure.

Since we use miniature marshmallows, building a solid frame is no easy feat. We need a wide base to get proper support for the rest of the structure, but putting a strong foundation together takes time away from building upwards. The trade off seems too time consuming until budding skyscrapers begin to implode.

We can learn a lot from simple marshmallows.

Just as a marshmallow structure needs a wide base for support, a child needs a broad base of learning to be truly educated. The challenges our children will face cannot be fully foreseen at this time, and so we prepare them as best we can for what lies ahead. Our building blocks are reading, math, history and the sciences, and we measure them out with generous doses of ethics, economics and excellence.

The children of today will soon own their own companies, raise their own families and make the laws that govern our society.

Maybe we should all pass around a bag of marshmallows and keep practicing with the small stuff until everyone gets it right.

# Sweet Traditions

I first met my mother-in-law at the airport, a few days before my wedding. She had brought along her husband, Tom, a small carry-on bag and a suitcase that required two people to heft into the back of my car. I soon learned that the carry-on bag contained all the necessities for her intended three week stay, and the suitcase contained food.

As a good Italian mother, she knew that she could not trust just anyone (me) to feed her son properly. She was going to see to it that her son had authentic Sicilian pizza and a cookie cake at his wedding, and that it would be done right, which meant that it would be baked in her own oven and transported from New York to Marysville, layered in wax paper and wrapped in Samsonite.

I tried to act as if people showed up at my house with edible luggage on a regular basis. One bite of her fabulous white pizza, and I swallowed my skepticism. But I was still puzzled about the cookie cake.

In the weeks preceding her visit, my mother-in-law had baked and frozen a variety of traditional Italian cookies. In short order, she revealed treasures that were familiar to Brian but new to me. She had packed almond paste cookies, biscotti, butter cookies, fig cookies and cream puffs waiting to be filled.

Food is an integral part of any Italian celebration or gathering, and cookies are often present. The cookie cake, actually a tower of cookies arranged on a pretty tray, is a special tradition.

To carry on the family tradition, our family constructed a cookie cake for a friend's wedding. We got to talk about family traditions from Brian's side of the family as we worked.

Tradition is the glue that binds generations through time. It isn't easy passing along a tradition that is still somewhat foreign to me, but I want to gather up the pieces of history that we can preserve and weave those fragments into a tapestry of tradition for our family.

While we worked, I told my children about the boxes of cookies my mother-in-law used to send. I told them how I was always willing to give up the entire tin of cookies for the few fig cookies that were included. Then one day a friend came over on the same day a box was delivered. I watched, silently, as he consumed almost the entire box of cookies. I nearly cried.

My mother-in-law sent boxes of cookies via express mail for several years. The boxes stopped after about a decade. I guess she decided that I could be trusted to feed her son. The last box she sent contained copies of all her recipes. And so, it is my responsibility to use those recipes to pass along a tradition. Some day, I will send my kids into the world with a cookie cake of their own. Later, I'll pack cookies in tins and send them through the mail, and each bite will remind my children of happy times spent together in the kitchen.

# Market Morning

It is market day, and the figs are ripe. The alarm is set for sometime dark, but I'm already awake, mentally preparing for the rush. I stumble into the kitchen, grab a cuppa joe and slip my sockless feet into Muck boots. On my way out the door, I grab Brian's denim shirt to use as a light jacket. The calendar says summer, but this morning whispers autumn, a cool breeze insistently turning to wind as I head out to the fig tree with a box.

I push myself into the arms of the tree, still-warm coffee sloshing around in my stomach as I navigate through the sticky leaves searching for figs. When figs are ripe, they change color subtly from a bright green to a softer yellow. The once-perky fruit begins to droop, heavy and tired. Many develop stretch marks; pregnant flesh anxious to deliver.

Across the field, the cows look at me, startled. They lie there, chewing their cud, trying to figure out what might be happening. My girls are creatures of habit and this is not, in their opinion, how the day is supposed to begin. Like me, they can't believe I'm up and out at such an hour.

In a few moments, the rest of the farm wakes up. My kids are out doing their chores early, and the sheep and lambs are not as cautious as the cows. A chorus of bleats threatens to overwhelm the suddenly urgent bawling of the calves. Turkeys gobble a welcome to my daughter who feeds them. Not to be left out, the ducks begin clamoring for a treat.

By now, my box is nearly full of figs, and the cows have determined that they may as well get up. Cookie ambles over to the gate, ready to be milked. Mocha follows close behind, each one vying to be the first to get a bucket of grain and the relief of an emptied udder. They wait patiently as Brian lugs out the milk machine.

I wash Cookie's udder, and we hook her up. The milk squirts into the machine, hot against the cool stainless steel. I go back to picking figs as Brian monitors milking progress. In a few minutes, the milking is finished. I take in my figs and go to collect duck eggs. One hand is dedicated to opening gates and picking up eggs. The other hand—the clean hand, if you will—picks more fruit.

I head in with a dozen duck eggs, my stomach full of figs, Asian pears, fresh prunes and a peach whose juice dribbled down my chin in the cool of the morning. I forget that I need to fix breakfast for the children until the whining begins. I wonder what sort of mother forgets to make breakfast. I send the children out to raid the trees for themselves and put some rice on the stove. We'll top it with butter, brown sugar and some milk, fresh from the cow.

The older girls have loaded the van, and they hop in with Brian to go to market.

Morning has begun.

# Lunch is Always Late

"Mom, I'm hungry. When are we going to have lunch?" The request for lunch comes throughout the day. To my boys, all meals are lunch, and in their opinion, lunch is always late.

The bottomless stomach of a boy does not come completely as a shock. My oldest son used to start looking for a snack as soon as the table was cleared. Granted, there are a lot of plates on our table so it takes a while to clear the whole thing. The poor kid had to go several minutes without food in transit from hand to mouth. My younger boys, though, may yet outdo him in the eats department.

Several years ago, our food intake was part of our homeschool schedule. With a little planning, we knew what to shop for and when. Great care went into balancing our diets so that junk food was offset by a dose of whole grains, veggies and protein.

I liked that schedule. After setting up a month's rotation of meals and snacks, I didn't have to think about food from day to day. When we focused on eating local, seasonal produce, I had to start thinking again, planning daily menus around what came from our CSA box, what we grew ourselves or what we purchased at the farmers' market.

It is trendy now to eat local food in season, and that is a good thing for many reasons. The local farmers' market and numerous farm stands provide many choices for fresh produce that tastes great, is full of nutrients and hasn't been shipped from across the planet.

For the most part, in our family we limit ourselves to the fruits of the season. In spring there are flats of strawberries and buckets of cherries that bring us out of winter and get us ready for a summer-long fruit fest.

One of our many family traditions starts each spring with the cherries. We stand on the basketball court and spit cherry seeds. Each attempt is duly measured and the champion seed spitter is crowned for the year. Watermelon season provides an opportunity to re-hone those skills and, perhaps, topple the cherry seed spitting queen. Every year, Brian reminds me that there may be a king someday just as I remind him that it hasn't happened yet.

In addition to the family bonding time, our seed spitting training sessions have paid off. A couple years ago, Bella won a bicycle in a watermelon seed spitting contest. The next year she went back to defend her title and brought home another bike which she bestowed upon a younger sibling.

You never know when a talent—however obscure—will pay off.

# Grocery Store Lessons

I used to take my children to the grocery store because I believed that each trip presented an opportunity for learning. We talked about our food. Sometimes I contrived certain lessons I wanted them to learn, like calculating the price per ounce of beef jerky in different-sized packages. Other times we talked about product placement and packaging. It took forever.

Several years ago, Brian offered to take over the grocery shopping. I resisted at first. Our lives are unconventional as it is, and telling my friends that my husband did all the grocery shopping only made them look at me funny. He insisted. He said it would give me a break. I knew he just wanted to sneak home with bags of those sesame candies he thinks I don't know about, but his persuasive arguments about saving me time convinced me. After a couple of trips with a helper, he had one stipulation: He shopped alone.

In time, Brian's shopping trips morphed into something more. Before he would hit the grocery store, he would join a friend for breakfast, sort of a men's morning out. Our children were even farther removed from the excursion.

As we all adjusted to the change, it was fun to see Brian get excited when toilet paper went on sale or to watch him become indignant when the price of a package of cookies increased and the size of the same package decreased.

I felt the occasional pang of guilt that he was learning these lessons without the children's participation, but it was offset by the thrill of staying home and having the week's groceries magically appear in the cabinets.

Oh, sure, I've set foot in a grocery store since Brian started shopping, but it has been for the occasional loaf of bread or tub of ice cream. It never seemed to count as real shopping. After four years of letting my sweet husband do the shopping, I went back to the store for a week's worth of groceries.

I noticed right off that there were few children in the store. I had that pang of guilt again, as I had not brought any with me either. I want my kids to know where our food comes from, so we grow a few vegetables, grow our own meat and gather eggs from our chickens. Still, we can't raise it all. In our lives, some things still come from the store.

No time to think of that, though, as I wandered blankly through the aisles, shopping list in hand. It was overwhelming trying to find everything I wanted in this unfamiliar landscape.

Many of the customers were using recyclable bags. I'd forgotten to grab Brian's stash, so I guiltily loaded up paper and plastic bags and headed for the escape hatch. We kind of make a big deal of using reusable bags at home, so I thought the kids might notice as they unpacked. They were too busy rooting around to see if I had brought home cold cereal.

By the end of my trip, I was again thinking of the benefits of taking the children to the grocery store as a learning opportunity. As involved as our children are with our daily lives, they need guidance to learn that fresh, raw food is more fragile than packaged food. They need to see us making budget choices as we consider what to purchase for the family. Children need to look beyond the packaging and advertising and learn to find the right ingredients to maximize their nutrition. They can do all of that at the grocery store.

I just hope Brian will take them.

# Preserving Summer

We call our lessons in food preservation home economics because I think it sounds more glamorous than the reality that comes along with long hours peeling, chopping and stirring. Even with all the work, I always have a lot of willing hands to pitch in. Tasting privileges carry a lot of weight around here, and cook's helpers always get dibs on what is in the pot.

Preserving summer's bounty is a hot, sweaty process. It is also a slow effort. We have time to take stock of what we have and to count our blessings while we work. There is much to be grateful for.

For example, nothing made me appreciate air conditioning quite as much as spending a week without the luxury. Ours died on a weekend, of course, right as we were canning tomatoes. The next day was the best. The temperature was moderate for summer, and we embraced this new adventure. Most of the children took long naps that day, and I contemplated living the rest of my life without air conditioning just for the peace and quiet it afforded.

The excitement wore off pretty quickly. It warmed up, and we found ourselves becoming quarrelsome more often, irritated at the smallest slight. My ongoing list of summer

94

projects got pushed aside in favor of searching for any place where a breeze might be blowing.

At times, I found it relaxing to sit outside in the shade. Conditions that might have seemed oppressively hot the week before now seemed tolerable, inviting even. I brewed some sweet tea, plunked some ice in our glasses, and we enjoyed a bit of rest.

Something about an ice-cold glass of fresh-brewed sweet tea just cries out for sitting in the shade talking with friends. The neighbors, if they saw us, took no notice. It seemed like it would have been so natural for one of them to mosey over (it was too hot to get up ambition to do much else) for a glass of tea. But it would have been out of the ordinary to sit outside together. I could have invited them, but they would likely have invited me in, out of the heat. Somehow it seemed like that would be missing the point.

I was sad for a moment. Our lives had gotten so busy that we did not sit around and chat as much as we used to. A drive through the neighborhoods in town confirmed that we were not alone. Perhaps air conditioning will one day be faulted with the decline of socialization and community.

Once the air conditioner was repaired, our lives returned to normal, and we finished up our efforts to preserve summer produce. For days after, though, I found myself wandering outside with a glass of tea, hanging out under the oak tree, hoping to somehow preserve some of the heat of summer to take out again on a cold winter's day.

Soon enough, it was time to tackle another project.

One year, while Brian was deployed, the older kids and I planted a couple dozen fruit trees. A friend set up the drip system so that all would be in place to surprise Brian when he got home. It was great fun.

That work really paid off as the trees moved into maturity, and we had a lot of fruit. My kids know the joy of picking a peach off the tree and standing there eating it, juice dripping everywhere. They also learned how to preserve some of the fruits and vegetables that are so abundant here in our farming community.

The time in between summer and fall is an especially busy time in our homeschool. A sense of urgency creeps into our lives as we deal with piles of produce while trying to get reacquainted with lessons and activities that follow the traditional school schedule.

The chill in the morning air reminds us that changes are coming and spurs us to prepare for colder weather. When autumn comes, I incorporate lessons about planning ahead. Together, the family cuts and stacks wood, works on a fall yard clean up, and, at the end of the day, we hit the sauce.

We really like applesauce, so when a friend offered to pick up apples for our family on her trip to a local apple orchard, you know I had to say yes. Our trees were still too young to produce a surplus, and we still wanted to have a supply of homemade sauce. The only problem is that we never really do things on a small scale around here. We bought six boxes and got ready for some serious saucing.

The girls and I undertook our task with all the efficiency of a government operation. We had a washer, a peeler and one person to core and chop. The jobs in highest demand had the coolest gadgetry attached. To keep the younger girls occupied, we created the very important jobs of Apple Transfer Specialist Level I and Level II. Transfer duties included moving the washed apples to the peeling station and moving the chopped apples to the pot.

In prior years, we had simply quartered the apples, cooked them and then run them through a borrowed cone-shaped food mill. This time, equipped with my new-from-the-antique-shop food mill of my own, I planned to stick to tradition. Then I came across an article about making apple cider vinegar.

We saved gallon jugs and bottles, and I checked several recipes. I was excited that we could add a learning opportunity to our fall ritual. There was a near-brawl over who got to put the cores and peels into the containers, averted only by the discovery that there were plenty of vessels to go around.

Brian was supportive of our efforts, taking a turn at peeling now and then and keeping the boys occupied. Both tasks involved a lot of hooting and hollering. The next day, things sobered up. It seems that the adults involved had forgotten a bit of basic chemistry. The vats of soon-to-be vinegar overflowed. Everywhere.

At this point, I remembered that expansion is an inherent component of the fermentation process. It would have been better to remember this when the children were enthusiastically filling the containers to the top with peels and water.

I checked my recipes, hoping for a clue, but all of them had general proportions, not specific information. It seemed fine at the time. The only warning they noted was to cover the jars with cloth to keep out the bugs.

Yeah, the bugs. Somewhere between the jug filling and the vinegar geysers, we were visited by a squadron of dive-bombing fruit flies, committed to their mission of invading my territory. The cloth covers did their job, and the wannabe vinegar was saved. After several months of waiting, we had one gallon of cider vinegar gracing our pantry shelf.

We could have saved a lot of time and mess by chucking the apples in without peeling, straining them as usual and buying vinegar at the store. But there was something in the process of learning, spending time with the kids and even letting them see me mess up that appealed to me. Still, I think I'm done with making vinegar. From now on, we're making applesauce the easy way.

# Iron Chef Homeschool

Come 'round our house on a typical weekday afternoon, and you will see our version of a reality show we call Iron Chef Homeschool.

Some days, I'm walking in as Brian is walking out. Suddenly we remember the question we've been too busy to ask all day: "What's for dinner?" The entertainment begins.

On the Food Network, Iron Chef America is a competition between a challenger and an Iron Chef. The show begins with The Chairman announcing the "secret ingredient," and the chefs then prepare a picture-perfect meal featuring that item. Our version is a bit different.

We quickly look through the kitchen, trying to locate anything that might be transformed into dinner. Brian is our Chairman. With a swoop of his arm and a booming voice, he announces the secret ingredient for the day. He then leaves to transport the girls to ballet, leaving me to prep a meal for my judges, a house full of hungry children.

Our support of a local farmer's Community Supported Agriculture program means we have a lot of secret ingredients. Farmer Jim has attained rock star status among our children, in part because he invited everyone out to the farm to see the operation and plant pumpkins.

My kids will try anything Farmer Jim has packed in the box.

True Iron Chefs and their challengers have an experienced staff of two sous chefs helping to prepare for competition. At home, we have a rotating assortment of cook's helpers of all ages who learn how to chop, measure and assemble while we work together. Once our line chefs reach age 10, we promote them to sous chef, an honor that comes with the responsibility of making dinner for the family once or twice a week.

True Iron Chefs have one other advantage I lack. TV chefs never contend with having toddlers underfoot.

If Brian is our Chairman, then Max must be our Alton Brown. He wanders in regularly to check on progress and ask what I'm up to, making comments about the ingredient list, my progress and totally unrelated topics, such as the shape of Barack Obama's head. I leave little piles of raw veggies on the edge of the cutting board, and Max samples his way through the kitchen.

The judging session—also known as dinner—commences when everyone wanders in for our meal. There is a flurry of activity as meals are plated and presented. On Iron Chef America, the judges might say, "I usually don't care for soup, but this surprises me."

Our judges are not so refined. They push their food around on the plate, then eye me suspiciously. "Are there onions in here?" or "Is that a bean?" Naturally, I never reveal my culinary secrets.

The grading is straightforward. Some evenings the judges look around hopefully and ask, "So, is there dessert?" Those kids will finish anything for a crack at dessert. I know I have a hit on my hands when kids clear their plates, ask for seconds or complain that a sibling got a bigger portion.

# Barbie and Fondant:
# A Recipe for Disaster

Birthday parties are pretty simple affairs in our family. Usually, the birthday kid gets to pick what we'll be having for dinner and then chooses a cake to go with it.

One year, Olivia she said she wanted a soggy cake. At that time, she still had a few developmental speech errors, so I asked her to describe it, hoping it would clear things up. I had no idea what she meant, but she assured me we had eaten soggy cake before, and we had liked it. She talked to me in that voice children reserve for parents who are obviously too daft to keep up. "Oh, Mom, you know, soggy cake." There would be no further discussion.

I was left alone with my cookbooks, my computer and my vague memories of what it was to be 5 years old.

I once made an "I don't know" cake for my son who could not decide on one type. It had several flavors of cake batter sort of swirled in the pan. It was pretty awful. Soggy cake had to be better than that.

Since I had more time on my hands than common sense, I decided to wing it again. The cake part was easy. I made a white cake from scratch and put some pink coloring into the batter. So far, my daughter was not impressed. We usually bake our cakes from scratch, so this was nothing special yet.

Then I had what I thought was an epiphany. I would whip up a batch of strawberry jam to use as filling, top the cake with a dome of chocolate ice cream and stick a Barbie in the middle so that the cake and ice cream served as her skirt. When we served the cake, the ice cream would begin to melt into the cake part, and that would count as soggy cake.

I should have stopped right there, but then I was left with the frosting issue. We aren't big fans of frosting around here, and Olivia has always been the pickiest of us all. Besides, I still didn't know if genuine soggy cake even had frosting.

Now it was time to consult a greater authority. I turned on the computer where I found a great idea on the Internet. Fondant.

The article I read explained that real fondant is difficult to work with, and it doesn't really taste very good anyway. Marshmallow fondant, the article continued, was easier and tastier. Olivia loves marshmallows. This had to be good.

Suddenly I pictured Barbie in a magnificent, marshmallow-infused ball gown, peering at me from her perch atop a soggy cake. She would be my Cinderella, and I would be the fairy godmother who designed a stunning dress.

The kitchen became off limits, prompting all of the children to suddenly need to come in for just one more thing. Nothing gets a child to pay attention like telling them to go away.

The fondant was fun, I'll admit to that. When the kids snuck in, they wanted to know why I was playing with Play-Doh. Maybe I need more Play-Doh practice, maybe fake fondant isn't as easy to work with as the Internet claimed or maybe draping fondant over an ice cream cake is a dumb idea. My Cinderella cake started to look more like a "before" picture than a finished product.

101

In the end, my daughter took it all in stride. She didn't want the fondant to touch the other part of the cake. She picked at her cake, leaving half of it to go out to the chickens as she usually does. It was a pretty uneventful finish to a grand effort. And then I heard it.

"See? You did make a soggy cake." I think it was a compliment.

# Part Five

## The Farm

Only he can understand what a farm is, what a country is, who shall have sacrificed part of himself to his farm or country, fought to save it, struggled to make it beautiful. Only then will the love of farm or country fill his heart.
~Antoine de Saint-Exupery

# Baby Chicks Signal Spring

If you don't think that one of the smells of spring is a cage full of baby chicks, you haven't really experienced life in the country. I remember boxes full of chicks from my childhood, warmed by a heating pad and an overhead light. They were a constant source of both noise and entertainment.

A few years ago, I convinced Brian that our own box full of baby chicks would be a welcome addition to our kitchen. I have no idea why he goes along with some of my ideas, but he does. I was especially surprised that he went along with the chicken caper given his background. Don't tell him I told you, but he has, shall we say, rooster issues, stemming from a long-ago incident.

That first batch of chickens we raised in the kitchen turned out to be half roosters. I thought it might send Brian over the edge mentally, but we ended up taking the roosters down to the feed store where we traded them in for a wagon. Such is life in the country.

I was more than a little surprised that Brian was the one pushing for a fresh box of baby chicks the following year. I think he said something about a good learning experience, but I was not sure if he meant for us or for the kids.

As the saying goes, some folks get up with the chickens. I am not one of them. Those kind of people apparently work at the U.S. Postal Service. The day after we placed our order with the hatchery, we got a call at 6:08 a.m. telling us our newest science experiment had arrived. Brian collected the chicks while the kids helped me convert an old drawer into a chicken nursery.

Alyona made it clear that she'd rather play with chicks than research them, but she grudgingly looked up a few things to satisfy an assignment. Then one evening we came home after a dinner out to find that three of our 25 chicks were near death.

Our daughter became an instant nursemaid, hitting the Internet for information and advising us all on how to properly care for her little patients. Fortunately, there is no CPR for chickens or we might have tried it. Soon after, they peeped their last peeps.

At some time during the chick rescue efforts, we realized that, like many experiences in life, reading the instructions before getting started might have been a good idea. When Alyona read the part about the chicks staying inside the house for five weeks, I felt a wave of panic. It was easy to remember the last time we had cute baby chicks in the house, not so easy to recall teenaged chickens.

Once again, Brian was right. Raising chicks turned into a great learning experience—for all of us.

After having some success with a small number of chickens, we felt like experts. Brian and I were ready to hatch the second part of our plan. We wanted to start a family farm, to provide an opportunity to be more in touch with where our food comes from. We added a couple of pigs and 150 additional chickens.

Often, I will assign research for the children to do. This time, Brian and I hit the books, looked up information about farming and invited unsuspecting farmer friends over for a meal so we could ask them questions until they politely found a way to escape.

Like us, the kids learned animal husbandry on the fly. Each day, they helped me prepare a bucket full of goodies for the pigs, then went out with Brian to feed, move pens and tend to the watering.

The kids enjoyed taking care of animals more when we worked together. The little ones had a chance to come along this way, too. The boys took special delight in the chickens. When Max was 3, he would follow the hens around, "Thank you for the eggs," he told them. "Thank you for your eggs." Atticus would parcel out grain, a single kernel at a time.

Soon, our flock of chickens grew again and we found ourselves with 300 chickens on the farm. After a little research, we decided to try and raise some worms to eventually provide a source of protein for our laying hens. I am a little squeamish, but I have a couple of brave kids in the bunch who volunteered to sort worms when the time came.

To get started, we found a worm farm where we could pick up a starter batch of red wigglers. The owner was kind enough to give us all a tour and relay a lot of interesting facts about worms. He started by asking the kids a few questions.

I was just about to tell him that our visit was an impromptu homeschool field trip when the strangest thing happened. All of the children were speechless.

He asked them about recycling. They just stared.

Undeterred, Kevin asked how long it takes to make topsoil. Silence. It takes longer than our country has been a nation he told them, but nobody wanted to volunteer how long that had been either.

Kevin asked what they knew about worms. Somebody finally spoke up and said, "Uhhhh."

There were a few more questions which Kevin ended up answering himself, as I held my breath and prayed nobody would tell him we homeschool. I had never seen them so quiet. I even had one hiding her face in my skirt.

Once they saw the worms, the kids started warming up. The face hider even peeked out from behind my skirt and whispered a few questions.

Back at the house, the little ones fought over who got to put the wigglers into their new home. For weeks after, as we turned the pile, my helpers were in there scratching around and finding worms of all sizes. They shredded paper and saved food scraps to take out and bury for the worms. You still might get a blank look if you ask them to define "biodegradable," but the kids can tell you what makes good worm food and what should be tossed in the trash can.

In the end, a few beds of worms were not going to be enough to feed the animals. It was time to grow again. This time, I had something else in mind.

# Udder Amazement

With a few months of farming under our belts, we were feeling pretty confident. We had successfully raised a couple of pigs and a few hundred laying hens. It was time to think bigger. Goats seemed to be a logical step. I really wanted a dairy cow, but I wanted to be sure I could handle a milking schedule. Getting goats was a way to ease into the commitment. Any surplus milk could go to the pigs. At the time, Atticus was having a great deal of trouble digesting cows' milk, so we also wanted goat milk for him.

In short order, we settled on a breeder and went to pick up our goats. Eight months pregnant, I lumbered out of the van and said hello.

Virginia grabbed my hand and pulled me a few steps down the path. "Here," she said. "Feel this udder."

The words hung in the air for a moment as I tried to absorb them. I am always talking about the benefits of hands-on learning, and this was a chance to really lay on those hands. The problem was, they were my hands. Book learning was starting to sound really appealing. Here I was, goat and breeder in front of me and my children behind me, watching to see if I was a woman of my word.

I had to do it. I reached for the udder. The poor goat was as confused as I was, and she was relieved to go back to her pen after I'd groped her. We continued toward the milking room.

I mentally went over how we had arrived at this place. Once we decided we wanted to add some dairy goats to our farm, we started our research. We decided on La Mancha goats and found a breeder who had a couple of goats who were producing milk. On the way over, I brushed up on my reading, starting with instructions on how to buy a dairy goat. Nothing in the instructions made any sense at all until I laid hands on a few goats. Even then, there was so much more to learn.

As we moved into the milking room, my children crowded around, eagerly examining a few newborn kids warming under a lamp. I had a lot of questions about the milking process. All we had ever done at home was pour milk out of a jug. This didn't look anything like that. The breeders patiently showed us all how to milk, and the goat chomped her grain and let us learn. It seemed so simple.

Though we had gone for two goats, we ended up adding a third goat who was set to kid in a couple of weeks. A baby goat would be a learning experience for the children I told Brian, but he knew the truth. Those babies in the box were just cute, and I wanted one. We packed our goats in the back of the van and headed home.

The next morning, we paraded out to the barn with all our gear. I had carefully disinfected the equipment ahead of time. With the children looking on, I washed Sweet Pea's udder, my hands, and anything else that looked like it needed a good cleaning. Sweet Pea was a sweet and gentle goat, and everything went well.

We brought Petunia in to be milked and repeated the process with her. Just as we were finishing up, she kicked just enough to spill out most of the contents of the bowl. For all our efforts, we were rewarded with a full half cup of milk with one black hair floating on top as a bonus.

The next few days had their ups and downs. Lily went into labor ahead of schedule. We started checking each hour. The last time we went into the pen, she started

110

pushing, as if on cue. Brian raced in to gather the children for an impromptu science lesson.

I wore a lot of milk that first week, but it got better in time. I learned when to move the bucket to avoid Petunia's routine kicks, and the girls learned to mix feed, bring the goats into the barn and calm them during milking time.

When we were picking up the goats, I was worried I wouldn't know when to stop milking. "How do I know when the goat is finished?" I had asked. "That's easy," Virginia told me. "The milk stops coming out." Finally, something was familiar. That part was just like getting milk out of the carton.

# Blow Dried Turkeys

With a milking schedule mastered, it was time to look ahead to Thanksgiving. We decided to raise our own turkey along with a few extra to sell. We ordered 70 just to be sure we had enough.

Around this time, I began to suspect that things happen to us that don't happen to most other folks. Take the turkeys, for instance. Brian went to the post office and picked up a box of turkey poults. Email may have replaced a lot of traditional mail services, but you can't send a box of poults as an attachment.

A poult, we discovered, is a baby turkey. They are adorable little birdbrains who, as we learned, love to swim.

By now, the kids had become proficient at helping me set up a brood box. Together, we cleaned the water jars, set up a little tray for food and strung up heat lamps. Everything seemed to be going as planned.

As this was our first time raising turkeys, I did some reading and learned that turkeys need help finding water. The solution is to dip each poult's beak into water when putting them into the brooder. Dip, dip, dip....69 dips later, I finished up and started in on the regular morning chores.

A few minutes later Olivia observed, "They look dead." It took a minute for that to sink in. I went to check and found a dozen turkeys soaking wet, lying on the floor.

Some were convulsing. They had found the water alright. They had been standing in the little rim under the jar, and now they were soaking wet and cold.

I did what any normal homeschooling mother would do. I called for back up. Immediately, I had a kitchen full of children pitching in to help. Brian plugged in a blow dryer and started blow drying turkeys. Someone brought in an extra heat lamp and power strip so we could add more heat to the box. We alternated between drying the turkeys with the blow dryer and rubbing them with a dry cloth. The turkey poults started coming around.

I called for marbles to take up space in the water tray. Now the turkeys could find their water without taking a bath. Things were looking up.

Then the power strip went dead, turning off the blow dryer and the heat lamps.

There was a lot of shouting at that point as we tried to figure out how to restore electricity to the heat lamps. Something was shorting out the power strip, but what? I picked up a heat lamp to examine the problem. Everything was plugged in. I switched it on and off a few times and the light came on. Funny thing about that bright light, though, it wasn't exactly coming from the bulb.

I realized that the heat lamp I was examining in my lap had caught fire, and I pitched it across the room.

The excitement soon faded. The kids went back to their morning routines, and Brian and I found time to have an uninterrupted conversation as we blow dried those turkeys. It was almost like a date.

# Socialization on the Farm

Life on the farm provides us plenty of opportunity to observe how other species socialize. It can be a little startling to realize how similar the barnyard is to the classrooms I remember from my youth.

Animals of any sort will do amazing things to be noticed. Male turkeys fluff up and fan their tail feathers. My son Atticus calls this "making a tom." The ritual is designed to establish dominance and attract hens. It isn't the strangest courtship ritual we've seen. Our billy goat pees on his head as a signal of his virility. The does swoon.

Many of our animals have an established hierarchy, not unlike that seen in human social circles. The term "pecking order" comes from how chickens and other fowl determine who is in charge. Low-ranking hens often have feathers missing from where the other hens have gone after them. Chickens who are in charge strut around the field and command the highest roosting spots at night. Those who are lower in rank sleep below with the lowest hens sometimes relegated to the floor.

Establishing social order in the pasture brings back memories of the dark side of school time socialization. There are more than enough bullies to go around.

Our turkeys turned out to be pretty interesting until they began getting aggressive with us. Initially, any aggression was contained within their ranks. From time to time, they picked out one bird who was not accepted by the flock. All of the turkeys knew who that bird was, and they took turns torturing him in various ways.

Male turkeys have a snood, a little floppy part that hangs down over their beak. It exists, apparently, as a target for other turkeys to latch on to. Once the aggressor has a good grip, the turkeys then run around the yard, squawking about as the others gather in a bunch and encourage them to fight.

If the designated pariah manages to escape, others in the flock will peck him on his way past, just to remind him of his low stature. We have had to remove a few birds to keep the others from killing them. Sometimes bullying goes too far.

I noticed a change in the turkeys' behavior when they were about half grown. Usually they would gobble a hello and come to see what I was up to. As they entered their teenage phase, a few of the toms tried to peck at me through the fence. Later, my daughter came to say that they'd been threatening toward her as well. Brian grabbed a shovel and prepared to establish the social order in a manner those birdbrains could understand.

To protect his family against rogue turkeys, Brian raised up the shovel while he stomped and yelled in the general direction of the turkeys. Those toms did what most bullies do when confronted with a real threat—they turned tail and ran.

Brian kept after them for a bit just to confirm, at least for the moment, his position within the flock hierarchy. Then he cleaned out the automatic waterer and filled the feeder. On his way back across the pasture, we could tell he had done his job well. As the toms huddled in the shelter, a line of lovesick turkey hens followed Brian back to the gate.

# Bonny

Up until this point, the idea of raising our own clean, healthy meat was only a partially realized ideal. The animals were all cute and fun when we started. We fed them, moved them to fresh pasture and watched them grow. All too soon, it was time to learn how to put dinner on the table.

"Daddy, why do we have to kill 'em? Can't we just buy meat at the store instead?" It was a good question, posed by a 7-year-old who was full of curiosity about everything. Brian explained, "Well, the meat at the store came from an animal, too." Hmmm, she hadn't thought about it that way.

It seems that a lot of kids haven't thought about it. Food, as they know it, just comes from the window at the drive-thru. For those who cook at home, too many kids think that a pork chop magically appears, shrink wrapped, chilled and set on top of an absorbent little pad that soaks up any excess blood. Milk comes from a plastic container, and fruit comes as a plastic-entombed roll-up. It isn't quite that easy.

My daughter Sophia, the one who wears a princess dress to pick slugs out of the woodpile so she can feed them to the chickens, seemed content with Brian's answer about meat. She was curious enough, too, to come out on the morning when Tom, the butcher, came to visit. We got an anatomy lesson right there, one we aren't likely to forget.

As our farm grew and took up more of our time, my concerns about curriculum were replaced by worries about farm life. Sometimes we've missed activities because the animals need our care. Our chore time increased as our field trips almost disappeared. I second guess the process, the value of teaching this to our children. Some days, though, it all comes together.

Math lessons went out the window some days as we made time for chores, but I realized, as we went through our morning routines, how much the kids were learning. Mixing bottles for the calves, building pasture pens and running fences all require measurement. We had lessons in volume, area and perimeter, right here in real life. Pride replaced worry as I saw the concepts sink in.

People worry that homeschooled kids will turn into some freakishly strange, unsocialized creatures. Worrying that my children won't be able to socialize isn't even on my radar. Like many of our adventures before this one, farming has turned into an opportunity to meet and interact with a variety of people.

The neighbors started visiting more often, perhaps to keep an eye on us. "My mom sent me over," my neighbor told me one evening. "She said you might be getting a donkey, so she told me to come see what is going on over here."

Of course we got a donkey. Bonny the Burro joined our little farm one Father's Day to begin her career as a livestock guardian. Brian is the only person we know who got a donkey for Father's Day, a fitting present for a man who got me hoof trimmers for the goats on Mother's Day.

Whoever says that romance dies needs to spend more time on the farm.

# Family Life

Life on our little farm affords many opportunities for conversations about how life begins. The birds are out there in the field doing whatever it is that birds do. The bees are out there pollinating all over the place. The whole family life curriculum unfolds before our very eyes daily.

At 4, Max began wondering how babies come into the world. It started when we brought home the goats. We knew that Lily was pregnant, and we explained that she was going to have a baby. One evening, as Brian was getting ready to run some errands, Lily went into labor. He took the little ones with him, and the big girls and I knelt on the straw and watched. I prayed she wouldn't need any help, and I was glad when she handled everything on her own.

How that little buckling arrived was clear to us, but not so much to Max. He came home to find a brand new goat in the yard and asked, "So, where did we get that goat?" When I told him that the baby goat came out of Lily's tummy, he just stared at me, trying to figure out if I was joking.

A few weeks later, I had a baby myself. For the next three weeks, Max told everyone he met that a baby had come out of my tummy. He was so impressed with my accomplishment. One day he put his hand on my still-swollen stomach and looked up at me. "So who is in there now, Mommy?" he asked. Ouch.

The topic was revisited when Big Lily, our Milking Shorthorn, had her calf one January morning. The little heifer calf arrived at dawn, slipping out into the morning fog while we were getting our boots on. We raced out to find the newborn calf, still steaming, laying in the straw by her mama. Brian and I watched as she took her first steps then we went and woke the kids to come and take a look.

That morning, as they waited for breakfast, Max and Olivia discussed the most recent arrival.

"Did you see Big Lily's calf?" Olivia asked.

"Yeah."

"It came out of Big Lily's tummy."

"Yeah, I know," Max replied. "But how did it get out of her tummy?"

"I don't know." Olivia stopped coloring for a moment and thought it over. "Baby ducklings come out of eggs," she offered.

"Baby ducklings don't have calves," Max reminded her. For the moment, the topic was closed. They went back to their coloring books.

Soon after, I found Max playing doctor. Every parent wonders what will happen when the children go exploring.

In this case, Max had taken his Fisher Price saw and was attempting to cut open the stomach of any sibling he could find, looking to see if he could liberate a baby. He didn't have any luck.

As we had enjoyed success with milking our goats, I decided that I was ready for a family milk cow. After an extensive search, we found a sweet little Jersey we named Mocha. After having goats, Mocha seemed enormous, and I was a little afraid of her.

Mocha was "in milk" when we bought her. That is to say, she had given birth to a calf and was producing milk. We bred her and, as the time grew near for her to deliver, I stopped milking to give her body a chance to devote itself to nourishing the baby.

As my number one fan and protector, Max was always anxious to help me with farm chores. He was fickle in his responsibility, a common trait amongst 4-year-old boys. He would not go outside if it was too hot or too cold. His favorite chore involved sitting on a bucket, keeping me company. Keeping company is an important job he reminded me often. And so, there he was one morning while I attempted to milk Big Lily, our back-up cow.

We thought that Big Lily might agree to share the milk she was producing for her calf with us, at least while we waited until we could milk Mocha again. Our plan was to separate Big Lily and her calf overnight then I'd milk in the morning, my observer perched close by. This worked for about a month.

Then one day, Lily had a new agreement in mind. She would stop kicking me if I stopped milking her. After she gave me the first 10 kicks, I was ready to agree.

Walking back to the house with an empty bucket, Max put his arm around me. "Mom," he said, "when I get bigger, I'll milk Big Lily so you don't have to. And I'll save the bucket before she kicks it over, too."

Later that day we had a visitor, a neighbor girl about Max's age. She entered the house crying, nervous that the dog was barking. My little protector jumped into action.

"Don't worry about the dog," Max said, slipping his shoes on and heading out the door. "I'm not afraid. I can handle it." My little man was growing up. He can handle it, he said. The question was, could I?

# Fences

The first time a pig got out, Brian came in with a tale to tell. "The little guy went right through the gate," he laughed. The pig had seen Brian coming with a bucket of milk-soaked grain and figured out a way to run out and greet him. As Brian slipped into the pen, the pig followed along. Cute little guy.

Next morning, it was funny all over again. The third day, seven pigs got out, and Brian wasn't laughing any more. None of us heard him yelling, so the neighbor came over and helped with the roundup. That afternoon, Brian patched the gate.

For livestock, fences are mainly a psychological barrier. Most of our fences are made of field fence held onto posts using little clips. If they work at it, the pigs can dig under them, the goats and cows can push through them, and the chickens can fly over them.

In some areas, we reinforce our fences with electric rope or net. When the animals hit the fence, they get a small shock, just enough to train them to stay in a safe spot. The electric fencing is even less sturdy than the wire fencing. If an animal gets started going through, they may just continue rather than back off. The perimeter fence is an added layer of protection for the animals.

The animals do challenge their fences, but they rarely go through them. The fences provide a clear boundary and a contract of sorts. Stay in the fence, the animals know, and your needs for food, water and even companionship will be met.

As baby chicks grow, we move them out of the brooder and into the greenhouse. A few weeks later, the chicks will outgrow the greenhouse floor and will move to field pens. With age comes responsibility. Their enclosure will still protect them and we will still provide them with most of their needs, but daily moves to fresh pasture mean they will begin foraging for a good portion of their food.

In time, the chickens will be big enough to safely leave their field pen and we will open the door to a new world, a small area of pasture surrounded by electric netting to protect them. The first day we open that door, they will test their wings and run in circles, enjoying their new freedom. As they grow, they will test their new fence.

Thinking about fences leads me to thinking about kids. Fences, also known as rules, are in place to provide structure, to nurture and protect. Kids want to try out their wings, run in circles, and eventually take on new responsibility and challenge the fence. Just as we are grateful to those who help fence the pasture, we appreciate friends and neighbors whose caring serves as a social perimeter.

The hardest part of parenting is knowing when to open the gate.

# Death on the Farm

We are careful in how we name our animals here on the farm. For the animals we aim to keep, either as breed stock, pets or as dairy animals, their names are likely to sound like pet names. Dolly, Sandy, Snowball and Skippy are a few of the crew. Animals we raise for meat are either not named or are named with their purpose clearly stated.

Our first calves were Porterhouse, T-Bone and their French cousin, Filet Mignon. The pigs answered to Bacon and Sausage. Cheeseburger, Hamburger, Lunch and Dinner have each taken their turns munching grass in the field.

When my daughter complained that she wanted to name the calves something that she didn't like so that she would not get attached to them, Brian declared that the new steers would be named Broccoli and Cauliflower. I never could remember which was which and ended up calling them both Vegetable. They didn't seem to mind.

In every part of raising our livestock, there is the understanding that death is part of the process. A year into farming, Sophia asked why we didn't just buy meat from the store. That question opened up an ongoing discussion about why and how we grow our food. We explained that animals in the store had been alive once, too, and then she was fine with raising our own meat at home. It didn't make butchering day much easier, though.

We think we can control death on the farm, contain it in a neat little box. The butcher is scheduled to come out on a certain day so we mark a red "X" on the calendar and circle the date. Some animals we process ourselves. The children are not required to participate in any way, but Bella and Sophia usually end up plucking feathers, and they fight over who gets to eviscerate. The process allows for anatomy lessons for the kids and, at times, for neighbors or friends who stop in to learn.

Other times, we pack up the animals and truck them off to meet the butcher. In some ways, that is simpler. Either way, death on the farm is easier when it is scheduled, on cue, and when the animal was harvested to nourish another life.

It is nice to think we are in control, but death also comes at odd times, sneaking up on us, catching us off guard. Our Muscovy duck hatched her first clutch—a dozen fluffy ducklings. She was so happy to get off her nest that she didn't pay much attention to where the ducklings wandered off to. After she lost five of them—and they froze to death—we set out too late to save the others, but slowly, one by one, they died too.

One summer, we lost over 20 chickens in one day when they wouldn't cross a sunny patch to get to the water in the shady spot on the other side of the yard. A goat kid died soon after birth; baby chicks routinely get crushed by their brood mates. Sometimes survival of the fittest really stinks.

My kids know that death on the farm is not like death in a movie. On the big screen, the actor comes back next week or next month, now starring in another feature film. If a death on the farm is planned, the animal comes back in another form to our table. Unplanned, we dispose of a body. There is no return to life.

After chores one evening, Sophia came and told me that one of our Muscovy ducks had died. Muscovy ducks love eating flies, and we have them as a natural method of fly control. They wander about, fly over any fence we put up and generally make a mess of things. In the end, the benefit to drawback ratio is about even.

I asked a few questions about the deceased duck and promptly forgot about it. Two days later, I walked into the barn and remembered. She was lying there near the door. Our male duck, her father, was sitting beside her. I wondered how much he understood. Was he keeping a vigil? Paying tribute? Or was he just waiting? He snapped the flies that tried to gather on her lifeless body. I wondered if he was sad or just practical.

I trudged off to get a shovel. I thought about how life and death are so intertwined. There cannot be one without the other.

Death on the farm reminds us to appreciate life on the farm. Chicks scratch up bugs, calves kick up their heels and pigs lie sleeping in the sun. New goat kids arrive, and the joy of spring drifts in on the wind.

# Hope

By any measure of reason, I should have left her alone to die, but I just couldn't do it. Born in a downpour, the little goat didn't get as much notice as her cousins had when they arrived a week prior. Petunia was an experienced mother, so I gave her two doelings a quick check and went back in the house.

A day later, the twins were weak and having trouble nursing. Although we have explained to her numerous times that she is a dairy goat, Petunia starts a rodeo anytime someone comes after her with a jar in hand. Sophia and Olivia gamely held Petunia's legs as I milked her enough to make bottles for the baby goats.

By the third day, one kid had died and the other was failing, too weak to take much even by bottle. She would nurse on her mother briefly and then, overcome by exhaustion, collapse in a heap.

Not willing to give up so easily, I held the goat on my lap, pried her jaw open and put little dabs of yogurt on her tongue. The texture was great; it stayed in one place long enough for the goat's muscles to coordinate a swallow. We mixed vitamins and minerals into her yogurt and prayed that the goat would pull through.

The little goat became weaker, and she lost the ability to cry out. Unless I woke her up, she did not eat. Lifting her head seemed to wear her out.

She was always "the goat," to me because naming an animal is a commitment to its future. The goats—so far—have been for milking, so they've had fanciful names like Jelly Bean and Coconut. I couldn't commit to naming this kid because I wasn't sure this kid was committed to living. I prepared myself to let go by trying not to care. If she lived, she'd be just another goat.

I wondered, as I often do, what lessons I was teaching my children. Compassion is an important lesson, but it can easily be confused with futility. Perhaps there was a better use of my time and resources.

On the fifth day, I imagined that the goat was a bit stronger, and she rewarded me by finding her voice and crying out in a frail voice. My elation didn't last long. The next morning, the nameless goat was doing a version of a commando crawl to propel herself. She had lost the ability to stand.

Petunia was attentive if we took the baby over, but otherwise oblivious to her child's plight. She lounged with the other goats and tried to steal little Jelly Bean away from her mother.

In desperation, I fashioned a feeding tube and poured some of Petunia's milk directly into the goat kid's stomach. For the first time, she cried loudly. When I took her back to the goat pen, the little one sank into the hay and fell asleep.

The next day, she straightened her back legs. Soon, she was standing on shaky legs. We celebrated with another shot of minerals.

Then one night I knelt outside with my daughters, held the goat under the starry sky and coaxed a little more yogurt down her throat. In that cold, damp night, I forgot about economics and common sense. That night, we named the goat Hope.

# Part Six

# Family

The family.  We were a strange little band of characters
trudging through life sharing diseases and toothpaste,
coveting one another's desserts, hiding shampoo,
borrowing money, locking each other out of our rooms,
inflicting pain and kissing to heal it in the same instant,
loving, laughing, defending, and trying to figure out the
common thread that bound us all together.
~Erma Bombeck

# Reality Show Audition

$P$eople often ask me if I have ever seen a television show called *Jon and Kate Plus 8*. I haven't. Apparently it was a reality show about a large family. As a woman with a house full of children, I can't imagine taking time out from the mountain of laundry to watch another family live life.

Not having television, I am occasionally behind on the trends. By the time I heard of the show, it had already been canceled. This left millions of Americans wondering what goes on in big families. Brian and I joked about pitching a show idea to the producers of *Jon and Kate Plus 8* based on our lives here.

Usually, my editor comes up with headlines for my column. For our proposed show, I came up with my own catchy title. I thought we could call it *Brian and Rose Plus 7 Kids Still at Home, 470 Chickens, 8 Pigs, 7 Goats, 6 Rabbits, 5 Bottle Calves, 3 Cats, 1 Pregnant Cow and Maybe a Donkey*. I could not figure out how to put in the homeschooling part. Maybe I do need an editor.

My kids are natural hams. They would love the fame. Bella reads my column aloud, and the little ones count how many times they are mentioned. They remind me that I don't write nearly enough about each of them. And bring out a camera? The place turns in to a mob scene. Even the animals like to mug it up for the lens. I haven't caught the goats and calves reading the blog to find their pictures, but you never know. If I set up a computer in the barn, they just might keep track.

If we had landed a reality show, there would have been more than just child labor laws to think about. We often have a fighting free-for-all that erupts at chore time. Of course, nobody is fighting over who gets to do the dishes. The real brawls are reserved for who gets to gather the eggs, milk the goats or feed Big Lily.

Big Lily is the nurse cow, not to be confused with Little Lily who is the dairy goat. We almost got a donkey named Lily but decided to wait. I suppose then we could have called them "The Lilies of the Field," but it just seemed too confusing.

For the show, I proposed an interactive feature where viewers could help us make daily decisions about our family such as whether to hang out the laundry or throw it in the dryer. Maybe we could let the audience decide who cleans out the barn (I vote for Brian) or if the kids really need to know how to diagram a sentence. Viewers could vote on whether story time at the library counts as socialization.

Come on, Hollywood, give me a call. Just don't phone me at nap time.

# Bathroom Reading

I have always been an avid reader, but I don't really understand the attraction of reading in the bathroom. I guess I figure that if you need that much time on the toilet, you might want to call your doctor and make sure everything is working properly. Of course, if you are in the bathroom right now reading this, please do not worry. You've made it this far in life, another few minutes won't kill you. Probably. Remember what happened to Elvis.

A ban on bathroom reading does not work in a marriage because men are different. When we put an addition on our house, Brian was lobbying for a full library with a toilet in the center. I vetoed that one, but did agree to keep a basket in the bathroom stocked with appropriate reading fare. The unforeseen benefit to this plan is that the kids know where to put magazines, and all of them eventually make their way into the bathroom.

I like to read books and magazines on the couch, partly so my kids can see me reading. The newspaper is best at the table with a cup of coffee, though I confess I still haven't gotten over the switch from afternoon to morning delivery. I often read the paper in the afternoon, but it is not so much from protest as from practicality. The little ones nap after lunch.

Given my love of reading, I am always happy to see my children develop an interest in reading and writing stories.

They happily plow through books and occasionally fight over who gets the next turn with a book.

A lot of my reading these days is on the computer. I enjoy corresponding with friends by email, and I follow several blogs. I also am a part of an online writing community, and one night, as I was up late pretending to write, someone posted a request for information. The writer was looking for stories about changes people had made as a response to the recession.

It was late, and the skeptic in me had already gone to sleep, so I typed a few sentences. I explained how we started farming to save money on food and to know where our food comes from, and that venture turned into a business that involves the children. The next morning, I had a reply from an editor. I answered some questions and half wondered if it was a friend pulling a prank.

A few emails and phone calls later, it started to sink in. It helped, too, that the magazine commissioned a photographer to come out and take pictures of us.

The kids instantly liked the photographer and showed her all over the place, arguing about who got to hold her hand or sit by her at lunch. She stayed for several hours, took 800 or so pictures, and left, peeling my children off as she walked to the car. The younger girls proclaimed that they, too, would be photographers when they grew up.

We were all excited when the *Reader's Digest* with our family's story arrived in the mail. One more thing to read in the bathroom.

# Fun with the Telemarketer

I don't much care for the telephone, so talking to a telemarketer is really low on my list of things I want to do. Brian, on the other hand, rarely turns down the chance to strike up a conversation with anyone. After listening to the pitch, he starts telling a story and generally having a great time. The poor telemarketer has to ask to get off the phone by the time it is over, all hope of a sale gone, but somewhat heartened (we hope) by being welcomed in a friendly manner.

I try to keep all of this in mind when the inevitable marketing calls come. One evening I got a call with a survey about family life and parenting styles, and I decided I would follow Brian's example and listen before I said no. I would be the voice of homeschoolers everywhere.

The young man on the other end of the phone started in with his list of questions. "How many children are in the home?" he asked.

"Seven," I replied. There was silence.

"You have seven kids?"

"No, I have seven still at home. You asked how many children I have at home. I personally have 10 children."

"So you have 10 kids at home then?"

"No, I have seven kids at home."

More silence, then more questions.

"How many hours of television does your family watch?"

"Does that include videos, too, or only regular TV?"

He checked the form. "I don't know," he said, "it just says TV. It probably means all of it."

"I hate to admit it," I said, "But I think we watch an hour a day by the time you add it all up." I felt a little guilty. When we got satellite TV, we promised it would be for educational programming, but our standards had slipped in time.

"That is less than 10 hours a week. Are you sure you don't watch over 16? To be included in the survey you need to watch more than 16 hours of television."

"Well, I guess I'm out then. Sorry." I tried to sound apologetic, but I am not sure it worked.

"Can you just say you watch 16 hours a week? Isn't that close enough? We won't be able to include you in the survey if you don't say 16 hours."

"I don't have time to watch all that television," I told him. I started to list my responsibilities, namely raising those seven children he had asked about.

He wouldn't be put off so easily. I got the impression that a lot of people had hung up on him before I came along, and he was hoping to make this work. "It's OK, I can check on that later. I think we can still use you. Now let me see, how many meals do you eat together as a family?"

"Do you mean dinner? We don't always eat dinner together."

"It just says meals. I think it means any meal at all."

"We eat at least one meal a day together, usually more, but not always."

"So seven then? You eat seven meals together?" His voice was starting to rise into a desperate pitch. "You can't eat seven meals a week together, the list doesn't go that high."

"There are 21 meals in a week, aren't there? How can the list not go up to seven?"

I don't think he heard me. He mumbled something about getting back to me and hung up. After the call, I realized that Brian has had the right idea all along. Talking to telemarketers can be fun.

# Master Suite

Her face was flushed, her forehead crinkled as she ran into the room. "Mom! Mom!" Every question is urgent when it comes from a child. I looked up from the book I thought I had time to read. Clearly I was wrong. "Mom, do you have a master suite?" She looked at me expectantly and tried to catch her breath.

"Yes, I do," I said. For a moment, she was satisfied, then her face wrinkled up again. "What is a master suite anyway?"

I could always tell when Sophia had been watching television. She loved to watch design shows with me, but they made her a little sad, quite disappointed that our home has never looked like the vision on the set. Nobody on TV has crackers under the couch.

Advertising speaks to my children in an extraordinary way. One day when I was scratching through my purse trying to find my keys, Sophia informed me that if I bought the purse she had seen on television, I would always be organized, and I would have a place for everything. "Plus," she continued, "you would have room leftover for two full water bottles."

I asked her why I might want to put water bottles in my purse. She shrugged. I reminded her that my purse is kind of like her bedroom. It only stays organized if we put things in their places to begin with. The reference to her room was enough to send Sophia skipping out the door before I suggested that she start cleaning.

I have friends who brag that you could eat off their floors. Some days that is true at our house too. If you looked carefully enough, you could probably find a whole meal down there. We clean up, really we do, but with so many children, it can be hard to keep ahead of the mess.

My kids share the household chores, and they are not always focused on the task. I assure myself that they are learning how to keep a home, and that is the important thing.

"We need to fix our house up," Sophia said. "You know, like one of those shows." Oh. One of those shows.

When we broke down and got television, my girls joined me in watching the design shows. The designers talked about shabby chic. I have the first half right.

Our house doesn't look like anything you see on design shows, unless you count some of the "before" pictures. It is easy to get caught up in the transformations. Easy to spend time and money working on the impossible goal of a picture-perfect house.

See, we live in a home, and what makes a house a home is different for each family. For a homeschool family, a domicile must be functional and practical. With so many kids in the house, things need to be durable too. Survival of the fittest applies to furnishings.

Guests at our dinner table are likely to find an astonishing array of mismatched everything. There is a crayon mural on one wall of the dining room, compliments of my son. I thought about moving a piece of furniture in front of it, but I think all the pieces we have are covering up other art projects.

We have a globe on a side table and a world map in the kitchen. Art projects and penmanship pages get posted on the wall from time to time, over by the poster of World War II planes.

We strive to take our learning where we find it, one day curling up by the fire with a good book or digging in the garden, another day building a fort or painting a picture. My quest to provide opportunities for learning means we sacrifice designer style. Our bookshelves are overflowing, our craft shelf oozes supplies. The puzzles and board games continually escape their boxes.

Our house will never be a designer's showplace. It is something better. It is home.

# No TV? No Problem

To my children's dismay, I am not a fan of television. For many years, we relied upon an antenna to bring us whatever stations the wind might blow our way. Often, reception was fleeting, and we'd lose the last half of a show we had decided to watch. After many years of inconsistent reception, we opted for satellite television.

We told ourselves that educational programming would be a good addition to our homeschool. The satellite company offered a family package, and that sounded perfect. Documentaries, nature shows and a few cartoons thrown in would provide learning opportunities for the children. Plus, I would finally get to see an entire episode of *Law and Order* after the kids were in bed.

A few days later, Brian had buyer's remorse. "There is nothing good on," he said. "Maybe we should have gotten more channels." We stuck it out on the cheapo plan, though.

For a while, we overdid it. I liked the design shows right up until I realized they were leaving me with a constant sense of unease. I have no design skill, no question there, but too many of those home improvement shows left me feeling deprived of the latest trendy home fashions. I turned them off, but it was harder than I

141

thought it would be. Strictly educational TV would be the rule. We hoped.

We don't get to see whales giving birth or see lions in the wild, so seeing those events on television was a plus. However, as we settled into a routine of an hour or so of television each day, that hour began to dominate our lives. We quickly ran out of educational options. There was arguing over what and when to watch.

Seating arrangements were problematic too. Standing, talking, or even moving around drew shouts of protest from fellow watchers. Worst of all, there was the whining for just one more show.

After a while, we cut back. Then we started farming. I found that having an electronic babysitter meant I could finish up my chores outside without having to check on the kids as often. Some chores go faster without little hands to "help," so keeping them occupied for an hour felt like a necessity.

What I got in return was irritable kids and more arguing. The younger ones stopped climbing trees and playing on hay bales and started asking to stay inside. One positive was that they could tell me the remarkable benefits of a number of products available for purchase. I winced, knowing that if the commercials were that ingrained, a lot of unwanted information was finding a way into my children's brains. I started lobbying to pull the plug.

Brian agreed to three months without any TV. After that, we would evaluate the situation. I had the pleasure of calling the satellite company. If you are looking to lower your bill, get an extra receiver, get additional stations at a super-low introductory rate or just talk to a stranger for a very long time, I recommend calling to cancel your television service. The poor guy at the other end didn't know what to make of me.

"If your kids are fighting over the TV," he whined at me, "we can give you another receiver so you can have a separate television just for them." I explained that I didn't want more televisions, I simply wanted no television. Three customer service reps later, I finally got my wish.

Detox was brutal. Sometimes I missed the mind-numbing oblivion. Those days, we set out puzzles, games or craft projects and got busy. We made it, and we didn't look back.

# New Vocabulary Lesson: Date Night

I have found three sure-fire ways to get my children's immediate and concentrated attention. The first is to go into my room, lock the door, keep walking into the bathroom and lock that door. At that point, if I unwrap a candy bar without generating even a single sound wave, I am guaranteed to have a line of children clamoring to get in. Children can smell chocolate clear across the field and perhaps beyond.

Turning on the television is another way to find my children. Lacking satellite or cable television service, our TV is used solely for watching DVDs. The content of the DVD is unimportant. If I popped in a documentary on the history of paint, my children would sit, slack-jawed in front of the television, pausing only long enough to ask if a snack was available.

The third way I've found to get a child's attention is to utter the words, "I want to talk to your father alone." Immediately, my children remember a myriad of pressing topics they need to discuss. Ballet recital is coming up in several months, there was a butterfly in the garden last summer and it would be nice to have a friend over a week from Tuesday. All of these important issues need immediate attention, and they must be interjected into any adult conversation.

My quest for a half hour of adult conversation led me to rediscover dating.

It is important for us, as parents, to have a discussion that gets all the way to the end without using such words as "potty" or "please don't stick that up your nose." Equally important, we want our children to know that their parents—even as old and decrepit as we are—can still go on a date.

Even with the best intentions, date night doesn't happen very often. After all, dating is what got us into this mess. The first time we carved out a date night, Brian's announcement provided the opportunity for an impromptu vocabulary lesson.

At lunch one day, Brian told the kids, "I'm going on a date tomorrow night."

"With who?" asked one of the boys.

"With your mother." I was gratified that Brian answered appropriately.

"Oh." The boys thought this over for a moment then both chimed in together, "Can I go?"

"Nope. Dates are for Mom and Dad. No kids."

"But what about me? Can't I go?"

We immediately realized that it had been so long since we had been on a date that nobody remembered exactly what that meant. Like most children, my kids beg to go to summer camp. They love to sleep over at a friend's house. Often, the gang will spend hours outside building forts and playing house, pausing only for a random snack or bathroom break. These same children were moved to tears at the thought of being excluded from one dinner with their parents.

Brian saved the day by announcing a movie night to coincide exactly with our time away. Suddenly the tears dried up, and they couldn't wait to see us go.

Our first date out was a success. We talked about the kids, of course, and the various aches and pains that come along with advancing years and farm life. I cut up Brian's meat while he tucked a napkin under my chin. In the middle of the conversation, the server came by to talk with us. The interruption made me feel right at home.

# Play Ball!

One year we decided it would be fun to go to the mountains for a white Christmas. By "we" I mostly mean Brian. I start shivering when the mercury dips below 70 degrees. Still, I am usually up for an adventure. We packed up boxes of presents, a small artificial tree, some lights and enough food for a few days. The newly renovated roadside inn had a large two bedroom suite with a heater that didn't work and only a dusting of snow outside. It was an adventure alright.

Christmas morning, we started passing around the gifts. At that point, I realized we had left Sophia's stash behind in the rush to get the van packed. I tried to think of a gentle way to explain the problem. Sophia just shrugged. "That's OK, Mom," she said. "Now it will be like having another Christmas when we get home."

I remembered this event as I stood in the sporting goods section of the store, pondering baseball equipment. Sophia had been bugging me about a ball and bat for a while, but every parent knows that you can't buy a ball and a bat for just one kid and expect to have any peace in the family. For our brood, stocking up on baseball equipment was going to be a major expense. I put her off.

Aside from the financial consideration, there was the practical aspect. Just because we can almost field an entire team, I have to ask myself if we actually should. Any mention of reality had been quickly dismissed by my daughter. Baseball looked fun; therefore, we should play. It was hard to argue with such logic.

As her birthday approached, I started wondering about getting baseball gear as a gift. It would be, by necessity, a gift shared by all, and I didn't want Sophia to feel slighted. Her habit is to share all her gifts. I try to find something each time that can be uniquely hers. The younger children, awed by her generosity, give her fancy chocolates and gum. Sophia never seems to mind, even when her siblings have mooched all her candy. I didn't want to diminish her birthday, and yet I wanted to give something she had been hoping for.

I started loading up balls, gloves and a pink and yellow bat.

The next day, my little slugger opened her baseball gear with her usual enthusiasm. She passed out gloves and designated herself as the first hitter.

I was appointed coach based on my extensive experience. First, I played softball in junior high school. Second, I once sat in a skybox at an Oakland A's game. Third, I have a sister who likes baseball. I was the most qualified person in the immediate family, so I started coaching.

Batting practice led to a game of catch. I left the children chattering and tossing balls in the yard and went in to finish washing dishes. I opened the windows to hear the children shouting encouragement to one another. The younger ones squealed with delight as they learned to use their gloves.

As the blue sky turned golden, I tried to burn the image of that warm spring evening on my brain. These are the memories I will treasure. I gave my daughter a present for her birthday. As she often does, she gave an even greater gift back to me.

# Homeschool Dress Code

One of the benefits of homeschooling is the lack of a formalized dress code. Most days we look pretty normal, but the younger ones are subject to random bouts of dress-up. On any given day, I may have a race car driver, a princess and a ballerina studying at the table.

A few years back, a short trip to town ended up with an impromptu trip to the library. As I held open the door for my kids, I realized that one of the girls was wearing yellow rain boots, a pink leotard and a pink and purple tutu. This was topped off with a leopard-print hat and a boa. She was one happy 3-year-old, and she was thrilled to be learning at the library.

My occasional mortification aside, I generally take our dress code—or lack thereof—for granted. I might send a child back to their room for something clean every now and then, but my children generally pick their own outfits.

Several years ago, I bought matching shirts for our family as we prepared to travel to Russia to adopt for the second time. That purchase was the closest we've ever come to a school uniform.

We completed the adoptions then spent a few days at the Black Sea with the family. As we sat in the lounge awaiting our flight to Moscow, our facilitator received a

149

call. "Something terrible has happened in your country," he said as he turned on the television. We saw a grainy image that we could barely make out, and then our flight was called. We boarded the plane that September evening and flew back to Moscow, feeling vulnerable, not knowing what reception would await us in this foreign country.

In the aftermath of the terrorist attacks, kind Russian people lined up to greet us. "We are together with you," we heard over and over again. When we arrived at the U.S. Embassy, we were greeted by a vigil with rows of candles, flowers and crowds of Russians there to pay their respects.

Several days behind schedule, airlines resumed their flights. With mixed emotions, we donned our matching shirts, each with a large American flag emblazoned on the front, and prepared to return home.

Crowds at the airport parted, clearing a path for us to pass easily. Everywhere we went, we were pushed to the front of the line. Our flag T-shirts spoke for us, gained access and started conversations with strangers.

As we deplaned in Seattle, we went to claim our bags to go through customs. A roomful of baggage handlers, many of whom were obviously immigrants, stopped working and chanted "USA! USA!" as our family passed by. I could not hold back my tears as we walked through the airport. Our shirts didn't divide that day, the emblem of the flag brought us together as Americans.

I wore my flag shirt many times after our trip to Russia. Each time I remembered the day our family came home with each of us proudly wearing an American flag.

# Safe at Home?

Like any parent, I often think about how to keep my kids safe. Most of the time, that means cutting up grapes for a toddler or showing a child how to walk carefully with scissors. Some days, the irrational fears become all too real.

When our local school district went on lockdown due to threats made by a madman, for one very brief moment, I breathed a sigh of relief. My kids were safe at home. It would have been easy to be smug about keeping the kids out of a school building. That feeling might be justified except that our home life has not been without our share of breathtaking events, trips to the emergency room and scary lumps in the pit of a parent's stomach.

I also had to acknowledge pretty quickly that someone on a mission of destruction can strike anywhere, any time. We all carry around with us an illusion of safety that can be shattered at any moment. Even though I had carefully stopped and was following traffic rules, we still had a drunk driver run into our van full of children. We made it out without injury, but there are no guarantees we'll always be so fortunate.

There are days when I am proud to homeschool, days I wonder what on earth we were thinking and then there are all the days in between. When we learn about any high-profile threat to safety, national or local, we all get a reminder that our children are both vulnerable and precious.

151

Before I had children, we hosted an exchange student from Brazil. I still remember driving Paula to her first day of high school. I was overcome with a sense of responsibility that I had not known before. I wondered not only if she would be physically safe in her year with us, but also if she would feel accepted by her peers. I could not imagine how brave her parents were to let her go.

When I stood in a courtroom in Russia and listened to a translator tell me that the judge had declared me fit to be a parent, I felt joy, but also anxiety. How could I be a parent with no instruction booklet to follow? Would I be able to keep my children safe from all the pitfalls of this world? When we returned again and our family was stranded in Moscow for several days following the September 11 tragedy that befell our country, my courage faltered as I wondered how I could possibly protect my family from random acts of violence.

The first time we welcomed a newborn child into our family, I didn't lose sleep over 2 a.m. feedings as much as I couldn't sleep for the fear. If I closed my eyes for one second, I thought, something unspeakable might happen. It took a while to consider that sleep deprivation might be clouding my judgment. I tried not to think about what boogey men, real and imagined, might be in our future. I felt that as long as she was in my arms, she was safe. For one peaceful moment, we were secure.

It takes courage to watch our kids venture out on their own—the first bike ride around the block, the first solo drive in the family car, the first job, the first apartment—so many firsts. Letting go doesn't get much easier when we learn about threats we've not yet imagined. We remember that parenting is not for sissies.

No situation, no event, no place, no child comes with a warranty. Parents everywhere know that all we can manage is to do the best we can. We say our prayers, hug our kids when they venture out into the world and hope that everyone everywhere makes the right choices.

# Temper Tantrum

At 2 years of age, she bristled with independence. Every move said, "No, I can do it myself." And what she wanted to do was whatever she saw the big kids doing. One favorite activity was standing in front of the fan, yelling. If she stood just right and yelled loudly, Sicily could hear her voice distort as the sound waves scattered around her. It was great fun.

My girl had watched the boys do this often enough that she knew the routine. When she saw that the boys were occupied elsewhere, she slipped into my room and closed the door. This time, she had the fan to herself.

My daughter tried to turn on the fan, but the switch would not move. What she failed to realize was that the switch would not budge because the fan was already on.

Her problem solving abilities were straightforward. She cried. She screamed. She stamped her foot. "On! On!" she demanded.

I went over quietly and switched the fan off. I expected her to turn the fan back on and start the routine anew, but she did not. She stood in front of the stilled fan and yelled "Aaaaaah! Aaaaaah!" until she realized that her voice was not distorted at all. Sicily was angry all over again.

She began to suspect that I was somehow the culprit, and she shot me a look letting me know that she blamed me. Since I needed to defend my honor, I helped her start the routine from the beginning. We turned on the fan together, and the game began.

Sicily got it wrong the first time because her skills at age 2 led her to follow an exact sequence of events in order to complete a task. At her level of reasoning, the sequence was come in the room, slam the door, switch on the fan, make noise, giggle. There was no room for deviation from the rule.

That little exercise in frustration got me to thinking about homeschooling. Each year has been different from the year before. One constant in our journey has been that we have adapted. We have no prescribed, preconceived sequence of events.

At times, that is a hindrance. A solid routine is a good thing to have when changes in life bring chaos. And yet, flexibility and adaptability serve us well—as long as we have the discipline to assess our progress and catch up as needed.

Strict adherence to routine without pause for reflection and adaptation would have produced the same result Sicily had when she didn't get her way: crying, screaming, foot stamping. It isn't nearly as acceptable coming from an adult.

# Greenschooling

It came as a shock to me to find out that I am a trendy person. It has been a long time since I've felt like I'm going along with a fad, but here I am, part of the "in" crowd. I'm cool without even trying.

The homeschool thing may be part of it, but homeschooling is not what places me squarely in the center of hip. I have these quirks, these oddities, you see, that come in and out of fashion. I am green. That is to say, I do things that conserve environmental resources. I even teach my kids how to conserve. When I want to sound like conservation is a part of our curriculum, I dress it up and call it life skills or environmental science.

See, I like to reuse things. On purpose. For example, I put leftovers into old cottage cheese containers. Brian goes along with a lot of my crazy schemes, but this one really pushes his buttons. He says that if we hide our food in old containers, we'll leave our leftovers languishing on the shelf in the back of the fridge. Plus, we won't be able to tell if we have cottage cheese or leftovers in the container.

I try to explain that we can tell that by opening the lid of the container, but he gives me that blank look the kids get when I ask whose turn it is to feed the cat. The kids get it though. We've made a quilt from old dresses, a chicken coop from old fence boards and crafts from whatever we find lying around. One day my daughter brought me an old pair of jeans the rag bag would have rejected and said, "Hey, Mom, can you make anything out of this?"

I prefer to say that I like to recycle, but the real truth is I'm cheap. And there's another problem. Frugality is in style now too. My cool factor is multiplying by the minute. I can't stop it. Officially, we are studying economics and environmental science. Sounds important, and it is. It just isn't fancy.

Thrift is in, and there are many tips on saving greenbacks. Several blogs buzz about making laundry soap. We perfected the technique a long time ago. We hang our clothes on the clothesline, too. My kids don't get too excited about that task, but I like being outside in the morning. We remind ourselves that our small efforts save money for other things. I try to make going out for ice cream or taking a trip to the beach one of the fun things we get to do with our savings.

Our environmental science studies don't always work out as planned. I couldn't think of anything creative to do with a ripped trampoline, so it took a trip to the landfill. I often forget to take the cloth bags with me when I go to the store. And sometimes the leftovers in old cottage cheese containers really do languish in the back of the fridge. At least then we can check them for mold and count it as a science project.

# Learning a Process of Nature and Nurture

"Hey, Mom, what is college?" Sophia asked.

"College is where you go when you finish high school," I told her.

She thought about it for a minute and asked, "Am I in high school?"

"No, honey, you gotta finish kindergarten first."

My daughter seemed happy enough with that answer, and she skipped off, content for the moment to be a kindergartener.

A year later, that same daughter announced, "My name means wisdom. I'm gonna be a wise girl." She confidently flipped her hair before asking, "What does 'wise' mean anyway?"

It's funny, the way children hear things and learn about our world. They haven't yet developed a set of expectations about how things should be, so they fill in the blanks their own way. Although it seems they can flip a switch and tune in or tune out, they are very successful at acquiring new information. They want to understand their place in the world, their relationship to everyone and everything around them.

When she was in first grade, Bella bounced into the kitchen one afternoon. "Hey, Mom, I learned about adjectives today." I stopped making dinner to inquire further.

"What's an adjective?" I asked, wondering if she could supply a definition. She thought for a moment and then replied, "Hot." She was gone before I could acknowledge that she had, in fact, named an adjective.

Here at home, we have regarded the first few years of school with a casual approach. There is so much to experience, it is hard to narrow the day down to book time. I watch as the kids feed the animals, spinning and twirling as they prance between pens, bringing water, chasing bugs and singing. We hope that learning responsibilities at a young age will encourage good habits in the future.

Habits—good and bad—lead to interesting discussions. As a family, we use the opportunity to discuss our similarities and differences and talk about what traits might be inherited directly—like blue eyes—and which ones can be learned from the environment we are in. Morning routines provide opportunity for the nature versus nurture debate.

When my alarm goes off, I always need a few minutes to think things over. Once I finally crawl out of bed, I like to sit, glassy-eyed, and stare into space until I can accept the reality that a new day has begun. My children are on my side, but is that a product of genetics or environment?

Brian is a rise-and-shine kind of guy, and his goal is to convert the kids. As part of this quest, he routinely encourages them to get up and get moving, not to settle on the couch with a blanket as they prefer to do.

"Hey, Sleepyhead, no sleeping on the couch," he reminded Sophia, then 4. She answers to a higher power. "I'm not sleeping," she said, rubbing her eyes. "I'm snuggling with God." That bought her a few days of respite from his reminders. How could he argue with that?

Brian's optimism may not have passed to anyone in the family, but he is undeterred. He also thinks he can put something down and expect to find it in the same place. One problem he has is that he tends to remember where he intended to put something, not where he actually put it. The kids share these habits, but they confound Brian's efforts to stay organized by playing a game we call "Confuse Daddy." The rules are simple—they put his things away when he isn't looking. Revenge of the sleepyheads is sweet.

# Veterans Day

When I meet someone I know has served in the military, I make a point of thanking them for their service. Sophia is the one who remembers, and she follows suit. She loves to hear about World War II and begs for stories of heroism. Brian and I try to talk about what patriotism means, each conversation or activity directed toward the age and understanding level of the children.

One year, the girls made cards for Veterans Day. "You can send them to your brother," I told them. Sophia didn't think that sounded right at all. "He's not a soldier," she said, "he's Edward." She couldn't quite wrap her mind around the idea that her big brother was a soldier, ready to defend our country.

I tried to explain it, but my own vision was clouded by memories.

I met my son in an orphanage in Russia. He wore a blue and white striped shirt and hugged me tighter than I'd ever been hugged. That first night, Ed woke us up at least a dozen times to hug first Brian then me. He was happy to be in a family, and he wanted everyone to know it.

My little soldier used to sit in the back seat of the car and conduct an imaginary orchestra using a banana as a baton. The first time he went to a sleepover at the neighbor's house, he came home mid-evening to give a report on how much fun he was having.

Edward announced his first career choice at age 9. He wanted to work at McDonald's because "they have those cool toys, and people come in and give you money." Soon after, he felt a draw to the clergy. After all, he reasoned, "You only have to talk for an hour, and then everybody gives you money." He was pretty focused on his goals.

As he grew, I saw signs that my son was becoming a man. When the septic tank backed up, he stepped up with the shovel. When the cat died, he got the shovel out again and dug the hole, trying to shield me from seeing her as the rain fell on us all and obliterated our tears. He helped with construction projects, fencing and more.

Eventually, Ed abandoned his earlier career choices and enlisted in the Army. He called to tell us he was heading off to the war in Afghanistan, and I wanted to put my hands over my ears and say "La la la la la, I'm not listening," as if that would somehow erase the reality. All that talk of sacrifice and heroism is easier to read about than to endure.

When he was younger, we read the stories, we talked about sacrifice. Now he understands the emotions Brian felt when he deployed and left all of us here. In living out the lesson, my son comprehends what he only read about before.

It is hard to imagine, more difficult to explain to my children, that heroes started out as everyday folks. They were kids who had dreams and grew up to live them. They showed up, stayed the course and gave their very best.

To my husband, to my son and to all the heroes who have served: Thank you.

# Olympic Parenting

Parenting may be the ultimate endurance sport. Coaches and spectators on the sidelines are in abundance, always with a word of advice.

The competition between Olympic athletes reminds me of the rivalry that often develops between parents. We size each other up at the park and at social events, often using our children's accomplishments as a measure of our success.

Mental scoreboards tally points and deductions, keeping pace with the conversation. Sending a child to college definitely awards points. Kids with bad manners count as an automatic deduction when friends get together.

I wonder what it would be like to have an Olympic announcer analyzing and broadcasting my every parenting decision. It might go something like this:

"It looks like she is giving the children cookies for breakfast. Now that is going to be a three-tenths of a point deduction right there." Would I get extra points if the kids made the cookies from scratch?

One day another mom told me that the only reason I have time to teach my children how to do chores is because we homeschool. She explained why her children were not required to help around the house. "With soccer, the tutor and dance after school each day, I couldn't possibly ask them to do chores."

I explained that I am completely certain that with our genes, our children will likely not be professional soccer players or dancers. They will need to wear clothes and eat, though, so it seems appropriate to train them to do laundry and cook.

We both ended that conversation convinced we were doing the right thing for our children. Our Olympic parent judging system can be a little subjective.

Other parents aren't the only scorekeepers. The kids have their own point system.

Sometimes we manipulate our homeschool schedule so that we are in school when others are out. Christmas and summer breaks go more smoothly when kids are occupied, and the kids are usually fine with it unless their friends are out doing something more exciting. That Olypic announcer might say, "Rose is facing a tough field of competition. She did a good job planning the family trip, but will it be enough to overcome the math assignment in the minds of the judges?"

Parenting will never make it as an Olympic sport. The scoring system is just too difficult to define. Each obstacle course is different, each parent faces a unique set of circumstances making it impossible to predict where we will find common ground.

Still, there are victories to be won. When I came home one afternoon, Atticus, a toddler at the time, rushed to the kitchen and stood there grinning up at me. He had a limited vocabulary in those days, so he did what he could. He said "Wow!" several times while applauding my entrance. The scoreboard I keep in my own head flashed a perfect 10. In that moment, I had won the gold.

# Bike Repair

"What we need is a wench," he said. Atticus squinted his eyes and pointed at me. "There's a wench right there."

I wasn't the least bit offended. After so many kids, you can bet I've been called worse by now. Parenting is hardly a popularity contest. In this case, though, I knew my son's intentions were harmless. At 4, Atticus could not quite produce the /r/ sound so he either substituted a simpler sound or left it out entirely. What he wanted was a wrench, and I had one.

I am in awe of those folks who can take a look at a problem and come up with a mechanical solution. You know the type, the people who can take apart a broken engine and put it back together in proper working order. They keep all that spatial information in their brains and they just seem to know how things fit. I don't have a mechanical brain. Installing a nail in the wall to hold a picture is about the end of my construction skill, so holding a wrench is not something I do often.

The love of a child, however, inspires people to do amazing things. In this case, I was willing to try my hand at simple bike repair. It should have occurred to me that for anybody who had seven kids still living at home, the word "simple" never precedes any task. I never remember these things until I am half way through a project.

As soon as I started with one bike, the line formed to the left. In all there were six bikes to be doctored. Flat tires were the main complaint, and I reminded myself that a flat tire was not the most complicated thing to fix. This was true for the girls' bikes. Use the wrench to remove the wheel, pop the tire off, replace the inner tube, air it up, replace the tire. Easy.

Then the boys came along. Maybe they sensed that I'm not mechanical, and I would need help. Perhaps they were inspired by watching Alyona fix her tire a few weeks prior. Most likely, it was just because they were boys. My two little guys were kind enough to remove the tires for me in advance of my efforts. They used a couple of wrenches to do this then skipped off to play. The wrenches were missing for two weeks while all the bikes sat in a pile waiting to be fixed. The original nuts that held the tires in place were gone forever.

I might have saved time by packing everything up, driving to a bike shop and waiting for repairs, but I would have missed the moments spent with a crowd of eager learners. As I taught my girls how to read the pressure gauge, I thought of how hard it was when I tried to explain how to read a gauge on a page in a math book. As so often happens, hands-on learning just clicked. The risk of exploding the tire probably helped them pay attention.

I guess fixing a bike tire is kind of like riding a bike. Once you learn how, you never really forget. Distant memories took over. I used to ride a lot in the time before kids. I had forgotten that I knew how to fix a tire and put a chain back on.

Now I have passed those talents on to my children. They can't use this knowledge to fill in a bubble on a standardized test, but they can use it to do something better. My kids have a new skill, one they will use and, when the time comes, pass on to my grandchildren.

# Independent Adults

When setting goals for my children, I don't sit down with a list of state standards and circle the ones that I want to incorporate. We have, instead, a general course of study we hope our children will learn. I want my children to become independent adults who can plan for the future, solve problems, manage money and be able to run a household.

Sticking to a schedule is not a skill we have really mastered around here. Something always comes up to add some excitement to the day. It is hard to schedule around pigs that dig under a fence or geese that find an open gate. Flexibility is our friend.

That doesn't mean we don't try to schedule and plan. We make our lists and do our best to follow them. Sometimes we consider each child's strengths as we put together a plan. With a couple budding bakers in the house, all of us agree that we should give them plenty of opportunities to hone their craft and possible future profession.

Some kids change their life goals according to a current interest. That works really well at age 8, not so well in the third year of college, so we encourage exploration and discussions while there is still time to decide. My home is full of future teachers, surfers, chefs and politicians. For now.

Atticus has always been an early riser. Often, we snuggle and talk on the couch even before the rooster gets up to welcome the day. When he was 3, we had a talk about the future. I wanted to see how far he could plan ahead.

"What are you going to be when you grow up?" I asked him.

"Big," he replied, "like Dad," The boy is practical, I can tell you that.

"Well, when you are big like Dad, what will you do?"

"I'm gonna buy candy," he said. "I'm going to get five Mickey Mouse candies."

"Well, do you think you will have a job so you can buy those candies?"

"Yep. I'm going to have a job, and I'm going to touch the computer." At the age of 3, opportunities to touch the computer did not come up very often. They were lofty goals, to be big enough to buy one's own candy and to touch the computer without supervision.

Since he has often showed an interest in helping his siblings with farm chores, I asked Atticus if he wanted to be a farmer. Every parent dreams of passing along a passion in life. Atticus looked away and thought it over.

"I can't be a farmer," he said. "I don't have a hat."

"You need a hat?" I asked.

"Yeah, I can't be a farmer because I don't have a farmer hat."

He grabbed a book and started looking at pictures. The conversation was over for now.

Next time I went to the store, I bought the kid a hat.

# Resolving Conflicts No Easy Task

When Max was nearly 5, Brian began working with him, counseling Max on strategies for controlling his temper. An opportunity to test these techniques came most days in the form of his little brother.

Atticus is the brother born for adversity. If you have no adversity of your own, he is more than happy to supply a full measure. The kid will argue about anything. When I advised him that his birthday was coming soon he replied, "No it isn't."

"You are going to be 3," I told him.

"No, I not. I not gonna be free. I gonna be Atticus."

There is a certain logic in this. There is no one quite like that boy.

Like it or not, he did turn 3. When the day arrived, he was happy to receive presents and to finally achieve the privilege of chewing gum.

With so many children to shepherd, we have amassed a small library of parenting books and advice. Among other issues, such books promise to help us learn to help our children handle conflicts. In the books, it all seems so simple. Kids fight. Parents advise. Everyone hugs and makes up. Life doesn't always look like that.

An announcement in the newspaper raised my hopes again. The proposed class promised to reduce screaming and yelling. I kept reading and found out that the class was to help parents stop yelling. The irony was not lost on me at all—I was in my room taking a breather after losing my cool.

Taking a time out works for me, but it has always been hard to convince the kids. My boys assure me their issues are far too complex to settle by backing down. There are real estate issues to be settled. They will go 10 rounds over who gets to sit on the low swing or who gets to hold a package of batteries. Such territorial disputes must be addressed.

Each evening we have quiet time. In theory, this begins at 8 p.m. In quiet time, the younger kids go to their rooms to play together quietly. We hope it provides them an opportunity to wind down slowly and prepare to rest. Conflict often arrives, compounded by fatigue. When the yelling gets too loud, we go and investigate.

One evening, we got to see that Max was taking Brian's counsel to heart. As Brian went to break up the wailing coming from the boys' room, Max exploded out the door. Atticus, now in sole possession of whatever item had caused the fight, stayed put in his room.

"Dad," Max sobbed, "I did just what you told me!"

Brian knelt down to look him in the eye. "What did you do?"

"Well, I took a deep breath."

"That's great, son. Really good. Then what happened?"

"Then I counted to 10."

Brian hugged him. "Good, good. What happened after that?"

By now, Max had stopped crying. He was confident that he had done all he could do. He squared his shoulders and related the most logical outcome he could imagine. "Then I hit him."

# About the Author

Rose Godfrey and her husband Brian have been homeschooling since 1999 as their family has grown to include 11 great kids. Using her background as a speech-language pathologist, Rose draws upon everyday life to find teachable moments as they come. Her column, *Learning at Home*, appears in the *Appeal-Democrat* and is part slice-of-life, part homeschool news.

Rose's days are full of sticky hugs, sloppy kisses, wrestling matches, prayer and other assorted motherly tasks, all of which bring more satisfaction than she ever imagined. If she had any free time, she'd probably take a nap.